OVERVIEW

Overview
 Assessing Performance
A survey on performance management conducted by Development Dimensions International - a leading human resources consulting firm - found that over 90 percent of organizations use a performance appraisal system.

But, only half of the managers and employees surveyed actually considered their organizations' performance appraisal systems to be effective.

Appraisal is both popular and problematic. The traditional approach to appraisal adopted by many companies has some well-known flaws. The appraisal is:
- an annual event unrelated to ongoing work,
- limited to only the manager's perception of performance,
- characterized by safe ratings that are midway between extremes,
- incompatible with current working conditions such as telecommuting.

Example: Rick and his manager, Claire, share this negative view of appraisal.

This book is designed to help you to remedy these problems, and to bring appraisal in your company up to date. It will make appraisal a purposeful, ongoing, and effective process by describing the three stages of continuous performance assessment.

Stages of continuous performance assessment

Stage 1

The first stage of continuous performance assessment is planning. In this lesson, you'll discover how to link performance goals to performance plans in order to thoroughly explain the performance that's expected from the employee during the appraisal period.

Stage 2

The second stage involves changing from just an annual performance meeting to ongoing communication about performance between the manager and the employee. This means continuously monitoring performance and motivating the employee.

Stage 3

The third stage prepares specifically for the annual performance appraisal meeting by collecting data. You'll explore common performance evaluation methods, and discover how to use self-rating in the appraisal process.

This book will help you to overcome appraisal difficulties and perform this vital managerial act effectively.

Performance Reviews

Martin hates January. Apart from the weather, it's the time when he has to appraise all his team members. It's not a prospect he looks forward to, and neither do his team members.

Example: When Martin reminds Jean that it's appraisal time again, she's appalled. Both of them hate appraisals but for reasons they won't discuss with each other.

Jean: What a waste of time! After all that form filling, Martin calls me into his office and mumbles a few cliches. He shows me a few bland, inaccurate statements about my performance, and asks me to sign on the dotted line.

Martin: If I can get away without anyone having hysterics, breaking down in tears, or slamming the door, I'll be happy. There's no way I'm taking any risks. I'm appraising everybody as average and hoping for the best. If I spend ten minutes on each of them, I'll get it done in a morning!

Martin and Jean are probably more cynical and disillusioned about appraisal than most people. But some of the attitudes they express about appraisal are commonly held.

Well, appraisal isn't a waste of time if it's done properly. Part of the trouble with Martin and Jean is that they don't actually talk to each other, and so neither knows what the other really thinks about the ways they go about appraisal.

Effective appraisal is built around a dialog, and Martin and Jean aren't even close to talking to each other. In this book, you'll discover that the best way to conduct appraisals is based on:

- creating a real dialog between the manager and the employee about performance,
- handling, not avoiding, employees who react emotionally to appraisal,
- using appraisal to really improve performance, so it's not a waste of time.

Complete this book, and the appraisal discussion will be a well-managed, productive, and beneficial experience for all.

CHAPTER ONE

Assessing Performance Continuously

Benefits of effective preparation for performance appraisal

One of the most common complaints about appraisal is that it's just a bureaucratic procedure divorced from the real work of the company. This type of appraisal is a once-a-year, form-filling chore.

Larry works in a company where appraisal is viewed as an unwelcome annual necessity.

> The human resources department sends the forms out in September, but I'm always too busy to deal with them until I have to. The return deadline is early December, and I think I can fill in most of the forms in a day.
>
> I haven't got time to discuss the appraisal with every employee, but I don't think anyone really looks at the forms as long as they're

completed on time. It's a nuisance, but I have to do it.

This is an ineffective appraisal and it produces ineffective results. It's ineffective because Larry sees form filling as the purpose of appraisal, and focuses solely on the need to complete this activity. Form filling should be the culmination of a planned process in effective appraisal. This preparation gives you time to develop the positive and useful aspects of appraisal, which will make it relevant and useful as a management tool.

Preparing for appraisal obviously takes time, and if you're already under pressure, this will be an added burden. But the results of this extra effort can be transformational. Instead of a perfunctory, bureaucratic chore, you'll make appraisal useful to you, the employee, and the company.

You can link individual performance to organizational performance

This makes the appraisal process feel more purposeful. It is no longer divorced from the real work of the company, but it's a part of the way that performance is managed in order to achieve excellence.

You can develop a process that involves the appraisee

In this way, appraisal no longer feels like something you do "to" an employee--instead, it's something you do "with" an employee.

This sense of participation makes the appraisal fairer and more balanced, as well as more effective.

You can devise appraisal methods appropriate to the particular employee
This makes the appraisal experience feel more relevant. Instead of a standard approach, you're able to individualize the process, and produce a plan of performance that's appropriate to each individual employee.

When managed correctly, appraisal is a vital management tool. When managed incorrectly, it's a pointless chore. This lesson will show you how to prepare effectively for appraisal and make it a positive force to develop performance.

Defining performance goals
Performance goals are at the heart of the performance appraisal process. If you fail to identify what an employee is supposed to achieve, how can you assess whether or not he has achieved it?

An essential aspect of effective appraisal is the preparation that every manager must undertake to make the appraisal correctly focused. Many managers assume that employees know what they're supposed to do, and give them space to do their jobs. But then, they face real problems when it comes to appraisal. As part of the process for preparing for appraisal, the manager must define the overarching performance goals that the employee will ultimately be appraised on at the beginning of the appraisal period.

This means that just after the appraisal meeting, the manager must begin preparing for the next appraisal period. In most organizations, appraisal periods tend to be for a calendar year. But whatever period is used in your company, you need to start preparing for appraisal as soon as the previous period has been completed.

Performance goals are fundamental to effective appraisal. Performance goals--sometimes called performance objectives--identify what an organization wants as an outcome from an employee. Performance goals are the targets that the employee's appraisal is based on. Poor or confused goals make appraisal meaningless. Defining performance goals correctly is essential for effective appraisal.

Company goals

Company goals set the context for individual goals. Individual goals should contribute to company goals. This will determine not only the activities the employee must perform, but also what the most important objectives are for the individual.

Job descriptions

A job description is a formal list of the activities that the job holder agreed to perform. It is usually created at the start of employment. A job description will enable you to identify whether a performance goal is a new demand being placed on the employee.

Previous appraisals

Previous appraisals should establish a track record to be used to set appropriate goals. From this information you can determine whether the individual is generally capable in her performance, or whether some goals might be difficult.

Examples of the ways that these factors have affected the determination of individual performance goals.

Company goal example

The company goal of "improving sales by 5 percent in the next fiscal year," meant that Rob had a performance goal of finding a new customer each quarter.

Job description example

Jenny's current job description doesn't include any role in recruitment. When a goal of "hiring an assistant" was suggested, she pointed out that this was a new role and activity for her.

Previous appraisal example

Jim trains students who have dropped out of his coworkers' courses. Jim's goal was only set at a 60 percent success rate, because he's training such difficult students. Last year, he was pleased with a 50 percent success rate. He's confident he can do better.

The three factors that affect goals

By considering company goals, job descriptions, and previous appraisals, a manager will be able to define effective performance goals for an employee. These performance goals can then form the basis of the appraisal process for the next period. Both parties will know exactly what the employee is supposed to achieve.

Align individual and company goals

Align individual goals with company goals. Company goals should cascade down. Focus on the goals at the level directly above the employee in question, and then allocate an appropriate element of that goal to your employee.

Review job descriptions

Review the current job description. Any new goal should be limited to a logical extension of the job description. As it's a new challenge, it must be clearly stated. The new goal must build on the current role, and not be an unrelated activity.

Review the last appraisal and set goals accordingly

You must review the last appraisal, and compare the projected goals with previous achievements. Goals must be both challenging and attainable to be motivating. A small increase on previous performance is normally effective.

Here are some examples of the ways that performance goals are derived from company goals, job descriptions, and previous appraisals.

Company goals

The company goal is cost savings of 15 percent. The marketing manager's goal is an equivalent reduction in advertising costs. Her assistant's goal is decreasing costs by placing the same number of ads with a budget reduced by 15 percent.

Job descriptions

A new goal to develop a new-hire training program would fit with a manager's job description that already includes training employees. The tasks are related because of the core training activity, so it's a logical extension of the manager's duties.

Previous appraisals

A previous appraisal identified that an employee in a call center had just met his goal of 25 calls per day. A challenging and attainable goal is to increase the calls to 30 per day. The most successful employee is making 35 calls per day.

Melissa, Billy, and George have defined performance goals in alignment with company goals, job descriptions, and previous appraisals.

Melissa

Melissa set a goal for each employee based on the company goal of cost savings. Her own goal was to reduce salary costs by ten percent. She set Will a goal of reducing the number of temporary workers used by ten percent, and set Ryan the goal of reducing overtime by ten percent.

Billy

An initial goal for Karen, an administrative clerk, was to produce a design manual. Her current job description did not require writing or design knowledge. Billy amended it to a more specific and appropriate goal: Collating information from each design team by week 45.

George

George set a goal for Brad based on last year's performance. Brad had just met his target of two new customers per quarter. George increased the goal to be ten new customers per year.

In setting goals for Chris, you need to align his goal with the company goal to sell personalized pens directly to the public. An appropriate part of the goal from the level above--yours in this case--defines his goal. Andy's goals stem from Chris's. For Eric, the anticipated goal should be a logical extension of his job description. Holly's performance in the previous appraisal period defines the way her goal should be set--as a challenging but attainable increase on last year's performance.

In this case, Elizabeth's goal of a bar-coding training program is aligned with the company goal of updating technology. It encompasses a relevant part of the goal from the level above her in the organization. Similarly, Shane's goal to facilitate the training is an appropriate part of Elizabeth's goal. Vince's goal logically extends his job description and relates comfortably to his excellent previous appraisal. Owen's goal relates well to his previous appraisal, and his target is a challenging, but attainable, 5 percent higher.

An effective performance plan

Appraisal can't be effective if all it does is take a snapshot of an employee's performance for a brief period, just before the appraisal interview. This is one of the most common faults with the traditional approach to appraisal that many organizations adopt.

Successful appraisal begins with a discussion between appraiser and appraisee, just after the appraisal interview, to plan the performance for the oncoming year.

The purpose of this discussion is to plan--with the employee--the details of what he should be doing in the next year, what successful performance means, and how it will be measured. This discussion produces performance goals, which are made up of two elements.

Outcomes

Outcomes are the products of the performance goals set for the employee--the employee's target for the next period, and how it will be measured. An outcome is a statement of a specific result the employee is expected to create or contribute to, such as "negotiate pay raise."

Standards

Standards outline what level of performance will be used to determine whether an employee has met and achieved the planned outcome. A standard will add information to an outcome. So, for an outcome of "negotiate pay raise," the standard might be "within the budget."

Effectively stated goals incorporate both outcomes and standards. **Examples of outcomes and standards that are then combined to create goals.**

Outcome 1

Respond to customers' requests for information about products.

Standard 1

Respond within five working days.

Goal 1

Respond to customers' requests for information about products within five working days.

Outcome 2

Produce 4,000 units.

Standard 2

Within 0.5 percent diameter tolerance per 40 hours machine time.

Goal 2

Produce 4,000 units within 0.5 percent diameter tolerance per 40 hours machine time.

Outcome 3

Develop customer database.

Standard 3

Testable version by week 25; finished version by week 40.

Goal 3

Develop customer database with a testable version by week 25 and a finished version by week 40.

The structure of a performance plan

When devising unique performance plans with employees, you have to create goals which incorporate some statements about outcomes and standards.

The statements about outcomes and standards are combined to create a performance goal. Each goal will be unique to the employee, and will incorporate some relevant parts of the outcome and standard statements.

Goal examples and explanations

Goal 1

"To improve quality of design by decreasing maintenance costs by 15 percent." This goal was set for a design engineer in a manufacturing company. All other costs are set to remain constant.

Explanation 1

This is a very poor goal. The outcome is vague and unrealistic in comparison with other costs. The standards are irrelevant--reducing maintenance costs is unlikely to improve the quality of a design engineer's work.

Goal 2

"Collate ethical policy guidelines produced by department heads within one month, and achieve acceptance within two months." The employee is a human resources assistant with a multinational organization.

Explanation 2

This is a mixed goal. Trying to include two outcomes is unfair to the employee--he can't control the work of the department heads. Good standards are based on time, but it isn't clear in "achieve acceptance" what must be accepted, and by whom.

Goal 3

"Reduce reprographics costs from their current level by ten percent in 12 months." This is an objective set for the manager of an administrative office with his own budget and reprographics equipment.

Explanation 3

This is a good goal. The outcomes are specific, controllable, and realistic in the context of the job. The standards are measurable, accessible, and appropriate as the office controls its own budget.

Case Study: Question 1 of 1

You are the manager of a sales department. To prepare your team members for their appraisals, you're working with them to devise a performance plan for the coming year. You begin planning with Alex, who is a supervisor on the accounting team. The accounting team has a team goal of reducing costs for the next fiscal year by 5 percent. Answer the following question.

Question

Alex's performance goal is concerned with supporting the sales team leaders in accounting matters-- specifically the budgets for the sales team members' travel expenses, which are set and controlled by the sales team leaders. What would be the appropriate standards and outcomes for Alex's performance plan?

Options:

1. Advise the sales team leaders on correct procedures for determining travel budgets four weeks before budget deadline.

2. Advise the sales team leaders on the correct procedures for determining travel budgets in a two-hour presentation.

3. Provide information, on a weekly basis, to sales team leaders on actual versus expected travel expenses.

4. Provide information, on an hourly basis, to sales team leaders on actual versus expected travel expenses.

5. Determine travel budgets for the sales team leaders for the next fiscal year.

6. Determine the travel budgets for the sales team members on a monthly basis.

Answer

In fact, standards need to be measurable, accessible, and appropriate. They need to be related to an outcome that the employee can realistically achieve.

Option 1: Correct option. The outcome statement acknowledges that Alex does not control the setting of budgets. The standard is one that is measurable in terms of time, and is appropriate to this performance.

Option 2: Incorrect. The outcome statement acknowledges that Alex does not control budget setting. But the standard is irrelevant and inappropriate to Alex's performance. Why should he inform the team leaders in a two-hour presentation?

Option 3: Correct option. This outcome statement is specific and clear. The standard is appropriate, and means that Alex can access the data easily and naturally.

Option 4: Incorrect option. This outcome statement is specific and clear, but the standard would demand a considerable and unnecessary amount of extra work for Alex in collecting the data.

Option 5: Incorrect option. Although the standard is specific, Alex doesn't have control over the team's travel budgets, so this would be inappropriate to include in his performance plan.

Option 6: Incorrect option. Although the standard is specific, setting travel budgets is the team leader's responsibility and is outside Alex's control.

The outcomes for Alex should be specific and controllable. They are to advise sales team leaders on the correct procedures for determining travel budgets, and to provide information to them on actual versus expected travel expenses. The standards that are applied to these outcomes need to be measurable, accessible, and appropriate.

This results in the following performance goals: to advise sales team leaders on the correct procedures for determining travel budgets four weeks before budget deadline; and to provide information, on a weekly basis, to sales team leaders on actual versus expected travel expenses.

When devising unique performance plans with employees, you have to create goals which incorporate some statements about outcomes and standards.

Essential elements of outcomes and standards

Specific

This means having a clear and unambiguous statement of the outcome. Both you and the employee must agree on it and have a similar understanding of it. The more specific the statement is, the better. Don't try to put more than one outcome in a goal.

Measurable

Standards must be measurable, so they must be defined in terms of quality (measured against a perfect standard), quantity (the amount produced), cost (a financial measure), or time (measured against a time limit.)

Controllable

The outcome must be controllable by the appraisee. If the outcome is dependent on the performance of other employees as well, this needs to be taken into consideration. You can try to limit the outcome to the part the employee controls.

Assessable

Choose a standard for which you'll be able to collect performance data easily and, preferably, naturally. You should not identify a measure which you will have great difficulty collecting data on.

Realistic

This means that the outcome must be achievable in the context of the organization and the way it operates. One way to ensure this is to compare it with other outcomes on the team, in the department, and in the organization.

Appropriate

The standard you adopt must measure something that is important and relevant to the performance of the employee. A standard that measures something that isn't central to performance invalidates the performance appraisal.

Performance planning is an essential component of effective appraisal. It defines the work that the employee needs to produce, and the way that her performance will be evaluated.

Special appraisal methods

Appraisal systems have been around for a long time. In some organizations, however, the approach to appraisal is outdated. Today's appraisal must be relevant to today's employee.

There are many ways in which working conditions have changed over the years. But when considering appraisal, two developments stand out - telecommuting and self-directed teams.

Contemporary working methods

Telecommuting

According to The Telework Advisory Group, more than 28 million American employees telecommute. This is working from home for some, or all, of the week, and communicating electronically with the main office. This needs a different supervisory relationship.

Self-directed teams

A survey by Dick Grote found no examples of performance appraisals on teams. He was referring to more self-directed teams, which operate with less management and supervisory involvement, and determine their own objectives.

As a manager, you must find ways of conducting appraisals that fit with contemporary working methods. Discover below how to appraise telecommuters and self-directed teams.

Outcomes

Outcomes are an important part of all appraisal methods. With telecommuters, you need to place even greater emphasis on outcomes as opposed to activities. If you rarely see the employee perform, you must be doubly sure about what results you expect from him.

Individual input

You must identify a mixture of team and individual performance outcomes that will specify the individual contribution of the employee to the team effort. You can't appraise individual employees purely in terms of team outcomes.

Communication

Communication is easy with the employee who sits next to you. But you must increase deliberate communication, initiated by you, with the remote worker to more effectively monitor ongoing performance.

Collaboration

A simple but significant outcome is the extent to which the individual employee has contributed to team collaboration. The key attribute of an effective self-directed team becomes part of the appraisal in this way.

Immediacy

Whenever you can, you must recognize performance outcomes, both good and bad, immediately. Remoteness can mean isolation, and lack of immediate feedback can easily result in an unnecessary negative appraisal.

Involvement

One technique worth considering is to involve other team members in the data collection and appraisal process. They will provide information about each other's performance. This must be a formal and open procedure to work effectively.

These four managers have adapted their appraisal methods to fit with telecommuting and self-directed teams in their organizations.

Find below examples of managers and how they have managed appraisal.

Allison
"I call my telecommuters every week, just to communicate with them really, but I also make sure that I know exactly what they've achieved in that week. I'm there to offer praise for good work and support if they're struggling."

Ricardo
"John, our designer, works remotely. His first appraisal taught me that as I wasn't involved with him on a day-to-day basis, I needed to be very clear about exactly what results we expected from him."

Kelly
"The design team works collectively, but each designer makes an individual contribution to projects. We make sure that when they plan the work, these individual contributions are noted and agreed on. We can appraise against them."

Tyler
"I've set up an appraisal system with the sales team in which peer evaluation is a recognized part of the process. Everybody rates

everybody else, and it gives me some really useful data that I wouldn't get any other way."

Activity - Defining Performance Goals

Identify performance goals for two or three of your team members.

1. Start by identifying the company goals.

2. Identify the performance goals for employees at the level above your team members. These should relate to company goals.

3. Apportion relevant parts of these goals to appropriate team members. You're aiming for a cascade of goals, all aligned with the company goal.

4. Review the job descriptions of the team members to establish whether the goals you are setting them--or other goals set in the past--are covered by the job description.

5. Ensure that these prospective goals are a logical extension of the job description. You should then amend the job description as necessary.

6. If the goals are similar, you can compare the goals you have set with the achievements of last year's performance goals. You should aim for a small increase in expectation to challenge the employee to improve his performance.

Activity - Defining a Performance Plan

Identify a performance plan with two or three of your team members.

1. Start by identifying the performance goals you have defined for them, and discuss a suitable performance plan with each employee.

2. Identify the outcomes--the results of the work--that you expect from each employee. Outcomes should be specific, controllable, and realistic.

3. Add standards to each outcome. Standards should be measurable, accessible, and appropriate.

4. Combine the outcomes and their respective standards into a series of objectives for each employee.

Planning for Performance Appraisal

One of the most common complaints about appraisal is that it's just a bureaucratic procedure divorced from the real work of the company. This type of appraisal is a once-a-year, form-filling chore.

Performance goals are at the heart of the performance appraisal process. If you fail to identify what an employee is supposed to achieve, how can you assess whether or not he has achieved it?

By considering company goals, job descriptions, and previous appraisals, a manager will be able to define effective performance goals for an employee. These performance goals can then form the basis of the appraisal process for the next period. Both parties will know exactly what the employee is supposed to achieve.

Appraisal can't be effective if all it does is take a snapshot of an employee's performance for a brief period, just before the appraisal interview. This is one of the most common faults with the traditional approach to appraisal that many organizations adopt.

When devising unique performance plans with employees, you have to create goals which incorporate some statements about outcomes and standards.

The statements about outcomes and standards are combined to create a performance goal. Each goal will be unique to the employee, and will incorporate some relevant parts of the outcome and standard statements.

Appraisal systems have been around for a long time. In some organizations, however, the approach to appraisal is outdated. Today's appraisal must be relevant to today's employee.

There are many ways in which working conditions have changed over the years. But when considering appraisal, two developments stand out - telecommuting and self-directed teams.

Continuously Communicating about Performance

Imagine trying to coach a football team when you only watch the last few minutes of a game. Well, that's what it's like if you see appraisal purely in terms of the annual interview between manager and employee.

In today's dynamic workplace, you can't assume that once you set your employees on a performance course, all they have to do is simply follow it. Work processes need to be flexible to cope with changing business and economic conditions.

When faced with unacceptable performance, it's a common reaction to look at the individual as the cause. But this isn't a productive course of action. The way you go about diagnosing performance will have a significant effect on the extent to which the diagnosis is accurate and leads to improvement.

Every manager who monitors ongoing performance will encounter some unacceptable performance. When you do, you can't allow it to continue until you have the annual performance appraisal interview. You have to deal with it.

Motivation is a key element in effective performance, and a lack of motivation is a significant factor causing problem performance. Consequently, every manager needs to consider the motivational state of all employees.

Recognizing motivational problems as causing problem performance is only one part of the equation. Now, you need to remedy the problem. As a manager, you can't make an unmotivated team member feel motivated. What you can do is alter the working situation--specifically the working situation that has caused the motivational problem--to remove or reduce that factor, and enable the employee to start to feel more positive about work.

Appraising performance continuously

Imagine trying to coach a football team when you only watch the last few minutes of a game. Well, that's what it's like if you see appraisal purely in terms of the annual interview between manager and employee.

Modern approaches describe appraisal as a continuous process, which creates a dialog between manager and employee about performance. By monitoring performance regularly, managers are able to keep better employees motivated and help those who are struggling.

Example: Candy holds the view that appraisal is a continuous process.

> There's no way I'm going to wait a year before I give my team members feedback.

> That isn't going to motivate them to work even harder, is it?
>
> Appraisal is a continuous part of my management role. I review performance constantly. That's how I know who needs help to perform even better.

The old-fashioned view of appraisal is that it's a once-a-year discussion between the manager and the employee. Obviously, this would not be the only occasion when the manager discusses performance with an employee, but this approach does tend to encourage less ongoing communication.

With this approach, managers could avoid some difficult and painful feedback, but they would also discourage some effective workers because of the lack of positive feedback. The newer approach is more effective.

The benefits of appraising performance continuously are that you're constantly aware of the performance of all employees on your team. This means that you can:

- identify performance problems at an early stage
- give feedback on performance to all employees
- motivate the employee who is performing well to achieve more
- support the underperforming employee.

Appraising performance continuously is the most effective way of managing performance. Monitor, improve, and motivate performance as a normal part of your everyday management duties.

Methods of monitoring and recording ongoing performance

In today's dynamic workplace, you can't assume that once you set your employees on a performance course, all they have to do is simply follow it. Work processes need to be flexible to cope with changing business and economic conditions.

Your team members will need to respond to these changes, and you need to know what's happening all the time if you are to be effective in appraising and supporting these employees.

You need information about the ongoing performance of your team members. You need to know about their successes and failures, and the barriers they have overcome. There are three ways to gather this information without consuming so much time that you can't do the rest of your job.

Meetings

This is a straightforward way of monitoring performance. You meet with the team, either as individuals and/or as a group, to discuss and review performance.

Performance logs

Performance logs can be any form of your own observations about the performances of your team members.

Status reports

These are formal reports from an employee to you indicating performance progress.

Vincent, Kristen, and Holly are three managers who see monitoring and recording performance as an essential part of their roles. They operate in very different contexts--Vincent works in a software company, Kristen is a social worker, and Holly runs a thriving jewelry business. All of them have found ways to continuously monitor the performance of their employees to suit them.

Below some examples of managers to find out how they monitor performance.

Vincent

Vincent has regular performance review meetings in which each team member updates him on progress. Any problems are resolved, and Vincent makes notes about the meetings for his records.

Kristen

Kristen supervises 15 social workers, and tracking what they're doing on complex cases is daunting. Kristen takes notes of even the most impromptu discussion about performance. Then, when she formally meets with her team, she is fully prepared.

Holly

Holly believes that the onus of performance monitoring should lie with the individual employee. She expects each employee to provide a weekly performance update. She has designed a simple form for employees to use that makes it quick and easy.

Many managers will use all three methods to monitor the performances of their team members. They can complement each other so that status reports and performance logs prompt meetings with the team or individuals. But each method has its own particular rationale.

Meetings

Meetings provide an opportunity for a face-to-face review. These are less restricted and more interactive than written reports. Some type of formal meeting should be arranged monthly, but there can be informal opportunities to meet your team members just by walking around.

Performance logs

These are your memory aids. A simple note--in a planner, on a chart, or in a file--even if it's often a quick impression of performance highs and lows, can greatly benefit you. The note can form the basis for either a meeting with, or a formal report from, the employee.

Status reports

Reports provide you with factual evidence of performance. They focus the employee on progress, and are particularly useful with remote workers. Make any report format short and specific to avoid time demands. A brief statement of progress over the week is often enough.

Example: Laura, Jacob, and Clare have all adopted a performance monitoring approach that works for them.

Laura: I supervise the furniture sales team members, and by far the best way to find out what's happening, is to see them in action. So, I walk around the floor so that I can have a little talk with employees about their performances. It's immediate and they can respond quickly. I'm not a fan of formal meetings--I think they stifle communication.

Jacob: As a call center supervisor, I listen in to over 100 calls a day. I've developed my own shorthand notes so that I can recall the individual performance issues that I need to follow up on. So, when I talk to my team members, I can discuss issues specific to them.

Clare: My team works on specific projects with a very organized set of progress targets. I've set up a system using e-mail and some planning software so that if their progress reports aren't posted on each target date, I can follow up on it. I expect their reports on time.

It's essential that you find a way of monitoring and recording ongoing performance in today's fast-changing business environment. Without this information, performance can easily spiral out of control.

Diagnosing the causes of unacceptable performance

Every manager who monitors ongoing performance will encounter some unacceptable performance. When you do, you can't allow it to continue until you have the annual performance appraisal interview. You have to deal with it.

The key to dealing with unacceptable performance is diagnosis. It's vital to be able to distinguish between the two major causes of problem performance because knowing the cause will determine the way that you deal with the problem. The two main causes are the ways the system may affect performance, and the capability of individuals to perform.

Causes of unacceptable performance

System factors

Work performance happens in a place and a context. It's part of an organizational system. System factors are beyond the control of individuals and are factors like poor workflow, excessive bureaucracy, poor communication, and inadequate tools or equipment.

Individual factors

Not everyone is equal and individual factors affect performance. With equal tools and training, people may still perform differently. They have differing individual aptitudes and capabilities. These are factors like motivation, commitment, knowledge, and logical-thinking ability.

In any working situation, you'll encounter people who are not working, or cannot work, as well as they should. Here are some employees from different departments of a computer manufacturing company.

Example: causes of unacceptable performance

Mike

Mike has fallen behind on the target for his team. The supplier of mother boards has had transportation problems, and Mike has had to wait because the delivery date has been rescheduled.

Cathie

Cathie's sales performance has dipped significantly in the last month. She's been offered a job by a competitor and is seriously considering the move.

Dustin

Justin has found the work on the assembly line hard. He's slower than the other team members. He just can't slot in the smaller video cards as quickly and neatly as his coworkers.

Adrian

Adrian trained as a graphic designer, and has set up his own web site. By exaggerating these experiences, he persuaded this company to hire him as a web designer. So far, every web page he has produced has crashed.

Melanie

Melanie hasn't completed her weekly balance. Her computer has been down for the last two days and she can't access the data she needs.

Katelyn

Katelyn tries very hard to keep her records up to date. But her supervisor made a spot check and found that she was using the wrong codes. No one had told Katelyn that the codes were being updated.

In these examples, Mike has a workflow problem, Melanie has an equipment problem, and Katelyn has a communication problem. These are all system factors causing unacceptable performance. Cathie has a problem stemming from a lack of commitment, Justin's problem is his lack of dexterity, and Adrian hasn't got the knowledge to perform well. These are individual factors causing unacceptable levels of performance.

Main causes of unacceptable performance

When faced with unacceptable performance, it's a common reaction to look at the individual as the cause. But this isn't a productive course of action. The way you go about diagnosing performance will have a significant effect on the extent to which the diagnosis is accurate and leads to improvement. Here are some useful guidelines for your approach to diagnosing performance problems:

- Discuss the problem. Don't tell the employee that you know the cause.
- Start with system factors. Starting with individual factors can make the employee feel like you're blaming him.
- Don't automatically assume that more training solves everything.
- Putting strong pressure on the employee to perform better isn't sensible if the problem is not her fault.

Example: Jack has learned from experience that diagnosing performance problems isn't effective if the employee isn't genuinely involved in the process.

> It's pretty easy to blame someone when things aren't going well. But you really don't find the cause of the problem that way. You need to talk "with" the employee not "to" him. I always start by getting him to talk me through

> the job. That way, I can find out if things that are my responsibility-like equipment and resources--are up to the necessary standards. My team members know that if there's a problem, I don't automatically blame them, and I don't enroll them in a pointless training course just to show that I'm doing something about the problem. I talk to them. Yelling at them doesn't work.

The best way to diagnose unacceptable performance is to enter into a dialog with the employee. No one knows the job and the circumstances surrounding it better than the employee who performs the task. Your role in this dialog is to ask questions specifically designed to elicit information that will point to the performance problem being caused by the system and/or individual factors.

Select each element to find out what sort of questions you need to ask the employee to diagnose unacceptable performance.

> **Structure**
>
> These questions establish whether working conditions handicap performance. Ask about the employee's reliance on coworkers and the way the work flows through the organization, identifying any relevant barriers.
>
> **Communication**

No one can perform if they don't know what is expected of them or how well they are doing. Ask questions about the information needed to do the job and the feedback given on performance.

Equipment

Equipment and tools need to be both available and reliable. Ask questions which establish that appropriate and up-to-date tools and equipment are on hand for the employee and that they perform as they should.

Attitude

These are questions about motivation and commitment. Ask questions to find out if the employee feels differently about the task in any way. Ask about changes in personal or work circumstances, which might affect performance.

Skill

Skills deficits may be a lack of natural aptitude or of training. Aptitude problems are identified if the employee can't ever improve his performance in comparison with others, or when a new skill is required. Usually, training can help bridge most skill gaps.

Knowledge

Knowledge requirements for performance are specified in the job description. Don't assume that the employee has this knowledge.

Identify the requirements and question the employee to establish that he has up-to-date and relevant knowledge.

The best way to diagnose all of the problems is to begin with system factors and cover each of the three elements--structure, communication, and equipment. Even if you discover that one element seems to cause the performance problem, you should still cover the other areas.

Performance problems are often multidimensional, so to ensure that you have a complete picture, consider all possible system causes. Then continue the questioning with a thorough examination of all the individual factors.

Case Study: Question 1 of 2

Scenario

You have identified that Sean is missing his monthly goals. Sean has always been one of your top salespeople, but now he is consistently near the bottom of the monthly standings. You decide to investigate the performance problem so you call Sean into your office to talk with him about it.

Answer the following questions, in order.

Question

Sean tells you that he knows he hasn't been meeting his monthly targets. How would you initially respond to him?

Options:

1. "The problem is that you're not trying hard enough."
2. "Is anyone else's work affecting your performance?"
3. "What's happened to your motivation?"
4. "Do you get all the information you need on the buyers?"
5. "Have you had any problems with the stock database?"

Answer

Actually, you should respond to Sean by discussing the issue, not telling him what the problem is. You should begin with system causes--not individual causes--and question him about structural, communication, and equipment factors.

Option 1: Incorrect option. This isn't opening up a discussion with Sean. It is telling him what the problem is. You're likely to miss getting Sean's perspective on the problem and risk misdiagnosis.

Option 2: Correct option. This is a question about a structural cause. It is best to begin with system factors. They encourage dialog with the employee.

Option 3: Incorrect option. This question is looking at individual causes. You should begin with questions about system causes. They are more neutral and encourage a dialog.

Option 4: Correct option. This is a question designed to establish a communication problem as a part of identifying the system factors causing unacceptable performance.

Option 5: Correct option. This question addresses the investigation of system causes by exploring equipment factors that might be causing unacceptable performance.

Case Study: Question 2 of 2
Scenario

You have identified that Sean is missing his monthly goals. Sean has always been one of your top salespeople, but now he is consistently near the bottom of the monthly standings. You decide to investigate the

performance problem so you call Sean into your office to talk with him about it.
Answer the following questions, in order.

Question

Sean tells you that the telephone sales team members haven't explained the full cost of the system to customers, so that when he tells them, a number of them drop out. This is what is affecting his figures. How do you respond to this comment?

Options:

1. "Good, so that's solved the problem. I'll speak to the telephone sales team members."
2. "Are there any other personal factors that might account for the drop in sales?"
3. "Do you think your selling techniques are working as well as they can?"
4. "Are you up to date on the technical details of the new lines?"
5. "You need some refresher training. That will fix everything."

Answer

In fact, you must continue to investigate the individual causes of Sean's poor performance, and not assume that more training will fix everything.

Option 1: Incorrect option. Assuming that there aren't individual factors in the problem performance without any investigation is ineffective diagnosis. You should check through the possible individual causes.

Option 2: Correct option. It's essential that you ask attitude-based questions to establish whether this is a cause of the unacceptable performance.

Option 3: Correct option. You should attempt to differentiate between an aptitude and a training issue in diagnosing a skill gap as a cause of the problem performance. This question does that.

Option 4: Correct option. Knowledge requirements need to be updated constantly in many jobs. Problem performance can be caused in even the most experienced employee by lack of up-to-date knowledge.

Option 5: Incorrect option. Automatically assuming that more training is required when faced with problem performance is poor diagnosis.

The diagnosis of Sean's performance problems should indicate the reliance on other workers' performances as a structural cause resulting from system factors.

But for a thorough diagnosis, it's essential to continue the investigation to include all individual factors such as attitude, skills, and knowledge, which might also contribute to the problem performance.

To continuously appraise your team members, you need to continuously diagnose any problems with their performances so that you can remedy them quickly and effectively.

Motivational techniques

Motivation is a key element in effective performance, and a lack of motivation is a significant factor causing problem performance. Consequently, every manager needs to consider the motivational state of all employees.

Some managers believe that paychecks provide all the motivation most employees need. But, although pay can influence an employee's job satisfaction, real motivation comes from the way the employee experiences his job.

There are four conditions which clearly affect employees' experiences of a job, and the absence of any of them causes the employee to become demotivated.

Conditions and symptoms

Achievement condition

This is the extent to which the employee feels that the job or task is complete and satisfying. Feeling successful will improve motivation, but if an employee feels that she can't be successful however hard she works, this will decrease motivation.

Achievement symptoms

Feelings of lack of success are often indicated by comments which describe a feeling of pointlessness about the work. Many employees describe the job as meaningless and want to extend the role in some way to have more of an impact.

Autonomy condition

This is the extent to which the employee feels he can do the work in the way that he thinks best. Feeling that you do the job in the way you want to will increase motivation. Feeling that the job is totally prescribed and not in your control will decrease motivation.

Autonomy symptoms

The employee who feels a lack of autonomy is likely to describe feelings of frustration about the control of the task, and will often criticize the current method of performance.

Challenge condition

This is the extent to which the employee feels that the job is stretching and demanding. Feeling that the job requires you to develop new skills will increase motivation. Feeling that the job is just repetitive and easy will decrease motivation.

Challenge symptoms

The employee who feels a lack of challenge in the job is likely to make comments about boredom, be dismissive of any skill requirement for the job, or be constantly demanding to do a new task.

Recognition condition

This is the extent to which the job results in feedback to the employee. Feeling that it will be noticed if you're performing well, or badly, will improve motivation. Feeling that no one will notice or that comments are routine and superficial will decrease motivation.

Recognition symptoms

The employee who feels a lack of recognition may make comments demanding attention, or comments that no one cares about his performance. In extreme cases, an employee may deliberately perform badly to gain attention.

Examples: Poor motivation affects each employee's performance levels

Achievement

Neil worked in quality compliance as an inspector. He encountered the same mistakes time and time again. His feedback to the team supervisors on common faults had no impact. His checking became more perfunctory.

Autonomy

Kate had to deliver the training session from her manager's notes. He insisted that she do it his way. She thinks it's boring to just lecture the new hires for 20 minutes. She wants to make it more interesting, but she just has to read the script. The ratings for her sessions have fallen dramatically.

Challenge

Danny administers the company pension fund. He checks for imminent retirements and sends a letter to relevant employees. It's a standard letter and the human resources files list the employees. He's bored and he isn't keeping up to date. He'd rather help his coworkers with their tasks.

Recognition

> When Carlos forgot to cancel the order, he expected to be asked to meet with his manager for a warning. Nothing happened and no one commented. He's missed the last couple of cancellation deadlines, and the company has had to pay out for goods they didn't want.

Performance can decline for many reasons. Often, a lack of motivation is masked by other factors-such as poor equipment, or reliance on other employees--which are easier to identify as causes of problem performance. But the impact of lack of motivation should not be underestimated.

If their respective managers had been listening, they would have heard comments from Neil, Kate, Danny, and Carlos, which clearly indicated not only that they were demotivated, but the reasons for this. Neil was feeling a lack of achievement, Kate wanted more autonomy, Danny needed a greater challenge, and Carlos felt unrecognized.

Examples: employees speaking to their managers.

Neil

> "No one takes any notice of my comments. The supervisors obviously don't give the feedback to the operators because the same mistakes are repeated. Inspection is more than fault finding. I want to get more involved with the operators."

Kate

"I really think the training lacks a bit of excitement. People are bored with it, and to tell the truth, so am I. I'm an experienced trainer. I feel I'm wasting my time trying to make this session interesting. It needs to be redesigned."

Danny

"Any fool can do this job. You only have to be able to read and count. What I want to do is to put it all onto a database and add in a mail-merge system for the letters. Developing an automated human resources system would be a real challenge."

Carlos

"I'm really sorry about the order I forgot to cancel. It cost us $3,000. I'd like you to double-check my work for the next few weeks. I don't want to make another mistake."

Conditions that affect motivation

Recognizing motivational problems as causing problem performance is only one part of the equation. Now, you need to remedy the problem. As a manager, you can't make an unmotivated team member feel motivated. What you can do is alter the working situation--specifically the working situation that has caused the motivational problem--to remove or reduce that factor, and enable the employee to start to feel more positive about work.

Achievement

The best remedy for a feeling of lack of achievement is job enlargement. This means linking the task to any other relevant task so that the worker is responsible for a complete piece of work - from beginning to end--with a definable final product.

Autonomy

Increase the extent of the employee's authority by removing all routine checks and reviewing performance on outcomes, not actions. This is useful with the experienced employee, who doesn't require close supervision, but less so for the inexperienced worker.

Challenge

Increase the demands of the job by delegating some of the low- and medium-importance work from higher jobs to the employee. This is particularly useful for the experienced employee who has shown consistently good performance.

Recognition

For an employee who is feeling a lack of recognition, you need to link feedback directly and immediately to both good and poor performance. Feedback must be accurate and detailed. Public praise may increase motivation if it's genuinely merited.

Motivational remedies don't necessarily require significant changes in working conditions. Sometimes all it takes are small improvements. Here are examples of some small improvements.

- Using the database an employee has designed can increase achievement.
- Being allowed to negotiate individual customer discounts can increase autonomy.
- Interviewing for new employees can increase challenge.
- A "good job" from you can increase your employee's feeling of recognition.

Here are some examples of the ways that some managers have altered the working situation to greatly improve motivation.

Motivational problems and their solutions

Jean

Jean had no sense of achievement as a veterinary technician, even though she loved working with animals. In the practice in which she worked, the technicians were responsible for a specific procedure. Jean was responsible for radiography.

The practice manager changed the system so that a technician was allocated several cases and supported them through every procedure.

Casey

Casey, an experienced clerk, wanted more autonomy. He was responsible for distributing and updating the parts catalog. A system was in operation when Casey joined the company and he was expected to follow it--reporting regularly to his supervisor.

The supervisor told Casey to devise his own system, which she would check quarterly.

Mary

Mary found little challenge in her filing job. She had been a filing clerk for three years. She was very capable, but boredom was becoming an increasing problem.

Her manager took the task of coding from Mary's team leader and asked Mary to code, as well as file. She had to learn both the coding system and how to apply it.

Ellen

Ellen's excellent performance was not recognized by her supervisor. She frequently worked on her own time to complete her orders.

Her new supervisor made a point of congratulating Ellen the next day when the order was shipped. He nominated Ellen for the employee of the month award.

Lack of motivation is a common cause of problem performance. The ultimate motivational force comes from within the worker, but as a manager, you can adjust working conditions to overcome the forces that demotivate.

Performance Assessments

Performance assessment is the part of the appraisal process where you start to evaluate just how good a job an individual has done.

Assessment is a crucial phase of effective appraisal, but managers can take a very different approach to it. Compare Bobby and Andy. They're both managers in the information technology department and both pretty experienced, but their approaches to assessment are quite different.

Effective performance assessment starts with data collection. Data on performance can come from a range of sources. Customers and self-ratings are some of the more obvious ones. But the key to effective assessment lies not in the variety of sources, but in recognizing the purpose of data collection.

An obvious and valuable source of performance data is that produced from a self-rating activity by the employee.

Who else knows the reality of performance better than the person performing the job?

By far the most common method of evaluating performance data is to use some form of rating system. Usually, the manager or supervisor will rate the performance of an employee using a numerical scale. This is a simple and familiar method used in many forms of assessment.

Systematic performance assessment

Performance assessment is the part of the appraisal process where you start to evaluate just how good a job an individual has done.

Assessment is a crucial phase of effective appraisal, but managers can take a very different approach to it. Compare Bobby and Andy. They're both managers in the information technology department and both pretty experienced, but their approaches to assessment are quite different.

Example: managers assessing the work of their staff.

> **Bobby**
> "I really don't know what all the fuss is about. I've spent the last year with these folks. Of course I know how they've performed--I just know it."
>
> **Andy**
> "I want facts and figures on performance. Usually, they verify my instinctive

> assessment, but I want objective proof before I say anything."

The systematic approach to assessment predictably involves data gathering, so that the facts about an employee's performance come from a variety of sources. But not all data is equally valid and accurate. Raw data has to be managed to be reliable. Self-rating by the employee is a useful source of information, but it has to be sifted to remove any of the obvious flaws. Data from other sources is often the product of a rating system. The limitations of rating systems need to be overcome for this data to be useful.

The difference between Bobby and Andy is fundamental. Bobby argues that he's got the data to make an assessment just from working with his team members. Andy feels the same, but he wants proof. By using a systematic approach to assessment, Andy:

- feels his assessment is objective,
- has the confidence to challenge poor performers,
- can legitimately give extra rewards to some employees.

Example: Follow Andy's more detailed explanation of his approach to performance assessment.

> One manager told me that if I didn't know exactly how well my team members were performing, I wasn't doing my job properly. I kind of agreed with him, but I don't think it's enough for a manager to say, "I know how my team members perform."

> Appraisal involves big decisions and I want to make the right ones. So, I'm not saying to one of my team members that they're not performing satisfactorily unless I have every fact and figure available to support that statement. And I'm not talking about bonuses to some team members unless I know they've really performed exceptionally.
>
> My team members know that the assessment is objective. It's my opinion, but it's based on all the available evidence. That objectivity is really important to me. My assessments are factual, objective, and accurate.

Systematic assessment is essential for effective appraisal. Facts and figures on performance need to be gathered and then sifted to create the correct evaluation of the performance of each employee.

Gathering data on performance

Effective performance assessment starts with data collection. Data on performance can come from a range of sources. Customers and self-ratings are some of the more obvious ones. But the key to effective assessment lies not in the variety of sources, but in recognizing the purpose of data collection.

Many managers think that the purpose of data collection is to provide proof of poor performance. This isn't the real purpose of data collection.

Like the perception that a glass is either half empty or half full, the attitude to data collection can be negative or positive. A negative attitude focuses on identifying poor performance and is characterized by blaming the employee. A positive attitude focuses on identifying good performance and is characterized by encouraging the employee. This is a fundamental difference. This positive attitude to assessment is in tune with the current perception of appraisal as a tool for improving performance.

Many managers say that they have a positive view of appraisal, but they actually approach data collection in a far more negative way. Data collection, to them, is still used to prove poor performance, and employees feel blamed by the process. You can avoid this problem if you're clear about the purpose of data collection.

Purpose of data collection

Standards

Data collection is used to measure performance against an agreed standard. This comparison is essential. By using this standard, you show that the data collection is neutral and objective. You're not judging performance, but merely measuring it.

Excellence

You're collecting data to determine excellence so that you can identify the factors that lie behind it. This allows you to support other employees to perform in this way.

Improvement

You're collecting data on problem performance to try to identify the factors behind it. Then, if you're successful, problem performance can be eliminated.

When the purpose of data collection is clear and appreciated, the process of appraisal becomes a positive experience for all.

Collecting data for the right purposes

Standards example

In a tire manufacturer, the assessment of office employees was very contentious. They said the assessment was arbitrary and subjective. When the system used on the shop floor was adopted - assessment against agreed on targets - the arguments stopped immediately.

Excellence example

The performance data on each employee collected by one software development company is discussed in detail at team meetings. Above-average performance is analyzed in particular. Other team members want to know what they can learn so that they can perform this well.

Improvement example

The owner of a small electrical contractor uses every problem as a learning opportunity. When his employees don't hit their targets, he knows that it won't be for lack of effort. So he wants to talk with them about what he's doing wrong that prevents them from performing better.

Data collection is at the heart of assessment and, consequently, at the heart of appraisal. Your approach to data collection will have a major effect on the whole process. A positive attitude to data collection leads to effective appraisal.

Overcoming false self-rating

An obvious and valuable source of performance data is that produced from a self-rating activity by the employee. Who else knows the reality of performance better than the person performing the job?

The most common problems with self-rating are employees who score themselves too high or too low. What causes them to make these errors? Are they deliberate, or accidental?

Scoring too high

There are two obvious causes for this problem. The first is holding an unrealistic and inflated assessment of oneself. This isn't a deliberate ploy. But if appraisal is linked to a reward, some unscrupulous employees will deliberately inflate their scores.

Scoring too low

The most obvious cause of this problem is that some people feel uncomfortable praising themselves, so they deliberately score low. Another cause is that some people don't want to be challenged by coworkers who might not agree with their assessments.

When employees are asked to rate their own performances, their responses can often be confusing. The employees that you think will give themselves a good score may, in fact, not do so, and the employees who haven't performed well may score themselves highly. If you can't predict how some employees will score, you can at least begin to understand why they've done so.

Example: responses to self-rating requests

Simon

Simon scored himself highly on all aspects of his performance. He really tried hard. In his mind, only faulty equipment and uncooperative coworkers stopped him achieving his targets.

May

May knows that she hasn't entirely met her targets. But she thinks that she can still persuade her manager to give her an overall rating of "excellent" and a bonus. There's no way she's going to score herself less than top marks on everything.

Ted

Ted scores himself in the middle of the range--any higher would feel like boasting. He knows that he's actually better than many of his coworkers--who score themselves highly--but he thinks that they're just exaggerating.

Karl

Karl isn't going to score himself anything more than average. That way, there's no chance that any of the other team members can laugh at him. He had enough of that when he got a merit award and they drew a halo above his head on the team photo.

Improving rating systems

Self-rating is too valuable a source of data to ignore just because some of the ratings might be false. There are two techniques that you can use, which used together, will eliminate false high and false low self-rating. The two techniques are:

- coaching your appraisees on filling out the forms,

- redesigning the forms.

In the design of the forms, you can enforce and encourage the truthfulness of the information, and eliminate some false high and low scores. This is a general approach. The design of the self-rating form does not separately target high or low scores--it eliminates both.

A better design for a self-rating form

Enforce truthfulness 1

Ask the employee to rate his performance against a measurable standard, such as, "increase sales by ten percent." This requires a response which can be verified. If you ask a general question, the response is likely to be far less accurate.

Example 1

Self-comparisons encourage honest self-rating by removing any competitive aspect to the rating. There is no rationale for unscrupulous exaggeration. Modesty doesn't matter when scoring against yourself. But comparison with others will still result in false scoring.

Enforce truthfulness 2

Score yourself from 1 to 5 on your performance in:

1. keeping costs within five percent of the budget,
2. transferring advertising to the Internet by the end of the year,
3. reducing employee levels by one full-time employee.

Example 2

Which area did you perform best in?

Score how well you think you have done in each of your major tasks by numbering them. Your best performance area is scored 1, your next best is scored 2, and so on.

Example: Andy and April managed to eliminate some of the problems they'd previously had with false high and low scores by the way they designed the rating forms.

Andy

Andy removed the general questions about achievements in core skills, and replaced them with specific questions about achievement of each performance goal. Each goal was defined by a measurable outcome.

April

April included a question in the self-rating form asking employees to identify which aspects of the job they had been most and least successful in. Then, she asked them to indicate the extent to which each goal had been met, as evidence.

Coaching should be specifically and separately targeted at high or low scorers. Deliberate, unscrupulous high scorers need to be warned. Unaware high scorers need to be counseled. Low scorers generally need to be reassured about the purpose of the process and how the scoring will be used

Coaching specific employees
Warning

You should explain to employees who inflate their scores - because of the possibility of reward - that their scores are only a small part of your final judgment. It will reflect badly on them if you feel the scores are deliberately inflated.

If an employee cynically applies for the customer satisfaction bonus even though she has customer complaints outstanding, firmly tell her that if she takes a similar approach to her self-rating, she'll be automatically downgraded.

Counseling

Employees who aren't aware that they have too high an opinion of themselves need gentle handling. Your approach should be to take them back to the evidence for performance, and explain why your assessment differs from theirs.

You may have a really eager employee, who always volunteers because she's convinced that she's the best designer, but you don't share this opinion. Prepare for the appraisal by asking her to bring evidence for all her high scores.

Purpose

Low-scoring employees who think a high score is boastful need to be reassured about the purpose of the self-rating. You must explain that it's for their benefit and gives them a chance to focus on areas of self-development. So, accuracy is vital.

For someone who is modest about his skills as a salesperson, be sure to tell him that the self- rating forms are primarily for him to identify what new skills he needs to develop.

Privacy

When an employee doesn't feel able to post an accurate score for fear of comments by coworkers, you must reassure him that the results are entirely confidential. The manager's final assessment score is all that will be made public.

You may have an employee who was named as employee of the month, but is wary because her coworkers were so jealous they constantly joked about it and mocked her. Make sure that she knows the self-rating forms are entirely private and only you will see them.

Designing the form is a general technique, whereas coaching requires personal knowledge of the appraisee and what might cause that appraisee to falsify the self-rating scores. Jess, Jasmine, Kerry, and Alex have used their detailed knowledge of the appraisees they are concerned about to target them with specific styles of coaching.

Examples: managers coaching their appraisees.

Jess

Jess was wary of Zac. She believed the bonus would determine his self-rating more than honest assessment. She told him that if she discovered any of her team members were deliberately exaggerating scores, she would definitely include the deception in her final appraisal.

Jasmine

Eric was new and eager to impress. He really seemed to think he was doing well. Jasmine explained his self-rating was a bit higher than her assessment. She asked Eric to bring the evidence to back up his assertions. Together, they could then discuss the performance.

Kerry

Kerry knew that Alice would never score herself above average. She always minimized her achievements. Kerry told her that she was going to allocate training support on the basis of the scores. She knew Alice wouldn't want to take a training course she didn't really need.

Alex

Alex had seen how embarrassed Vendela was when the other team members heard that she was employee of the month. He made a particular effort to tell Vendela that all of the self-rating forms were confidential. Alex wasn't sure that Vendela would be entirely truthful otherwise.

To overcome the problems of false self-rating, you have to attack on two fronts. First, you must improve the design of the self-rating forms. Avoid general questions and use standards-based questions. Then, with the addition of self-comparison questions, you can encourage and enforce employees to be more truthful. Secondly, using your knowledge of each employee, you must coach each individual employee with an approach that targets the cause of the self-rating problem specifically.

Improving the design of the self-rating form by basing the questions on measurable standards and by increasing the amount of self-comparison will help to remove a lot of the problems from the previous system, which resulted in falsifications. More targeted and specific coaching will help to eliminate even more problems.

Stuart has a genuine but false picture of his ability. The best approach, therefore, is gentle counseling, supported by evidence. Patty's embarrassed attitude means you have to persuade her that she isn't boasting. By emphasizing the development part of the self-rating, you're encouraging her to be more honest.

Even though false self-rating can devalue the results, don't give up on self-assessment. If you do, you'll miss out on a valuable source of performance data. It's definitely worth your while to resolve any problems with self-rating.

Redesign forms to enforce and encourage more honest answers. Recognize why each person may respond falsely so that you can coach each of them to give you the accurate answers that you need.

Improving rating systems

By far the most common method of evaluating performance data is to use some form of rating system. Usually, the manager or supervisor will rate the performance of an employee using a numerical scale. This is a simple and familiar method used in many forms of assessment.

But although rating systems are familiar and easy to use, they also have some notable limitations, which need to be overcome if they're to be effective.

These limitations become most evident in the workplace when rating systems are overused and taken for granted. Familiarity is a real benefit, but it also breeds contempt.

Examples: ways in which using a simple rating system can backfire.

Don

Don complained about his appraisal. His supervisor had rated him as well below expectations on the first item, and didn't seem to be able to make a fair judgment about Don after that.

Ellen

Ellen always scores her employees in the middle of the scale. People used to joke that she was naturally cautious, but now it seems to be a habit she can't break.

Leon

Leon refused to accept his appraisal. He said his manager had hardly seen him perform. Other people had told him he was doing well, but his manager had come on a bad day. It wasn't right that the appraisal should only be based on one person's judgment.

The simplicity and familiarity of rating systems are major attractions and the causes of many of their limitations. Because the process is entirely familiar to most people, they exercise less thought and diligence in the ways they score than they might with a system that's new to them. Such a simple method is easy to use, but it brings with it significant limitations.

Rating-system limitations

Impressions

Many raters make quick, impressionistic judgments based on factors other than evidence. A common form of this is what's known as either the horns or halo effect--the rater identifies a terrible or excellent attribute early in the process. This impression influences the remaining scores.

Inaccuracies

There are three common and persistent forms of inaccuracy. The two most obvious ones are raters who always score higher or lower than anybody else. But the third form of inaccuracy is probably even more common. It is raters who always score in the middle of the scale.

One dimensional

The one-dimensional limitation is a product of the simple way most rating systems are administered. In most cases, the rating is performed by only one person. This makes for ease of use, but also a very limited and subjective perspective on the performance being rated.

In spite of these limitations, rating scales are still commonly used as an integral part of most appraisal systems. Given this fact, it's sensible to consider ways to overcome the limitations, rather than attempt to find an alternative and equally simple and familiar replacement method.

Strategies to overcome the limitations of rating systems

Train raters

Train raters in the processes and skills, as well as in the paperwork of appraisal. Use experiential learning--role playing and simulations--to explore the rating process with coworkers. Enable raters to compare their results with others.

Use forced distribution

Insist on a forced distribution of the ratings so that it's impossible for a rater to score persistently in any form. The rater must distribute scores according to a formula so that there are always some in the top, middle, and bottom.

Use more raters

Increase the number of raters so that there's more than one contributing to the rating system--for example, a peer, customer, or subordinate. Use a behaviorally based scale which describes the detailed levels of performance to add another perspective.

Introducing some of these approaches - particularly developing behaviorally based rating scales - can be very time consuming. However, they'll definitely improve your appraisal system.

Examples of how the limitations of rating systems were overcome:

Janet

Janet insisted on a three-day training course for all managers conducting appraisals. She had video examples of employees to allow managers to compare and then discuss the ways they rated each employee. Her goal was consistency of appraisal.

Alan

Alan decided to use a forced distribution system in the appraisals. Many managers were uncomfortable with it at first. But as they used it more often, they said that it did, in fact, represent an accurate picture of the range of performances across the company.

Todd

Todd organized it so that managers used ratings from customers as well as other methods. It took him a while to persuade both the customers and the managers to work together, and information took longer to process. But the final appraisal was more balanced.

Rating scales are simple and familiar to use. These huge advantages mean that you must overcome any limitations they have, and use them effectively.

Learning Aid - Behaviorally Based Scales

A behaviorally based scale is a detailed description of all the ranges of behaviors you can expect from an employee in a particular area of performance. You can then score the employee in relation to the behaviors he exhibits. These scales are complex and lengthy to produce. Here is an example of one:

7	Always greets customers with a friendly "hello" when they enter the department, and always approaches them to offer assistance.
6	Often greets customers with a friendly "hello" when they enter the department, and approaches them to offer assistance.
5	Greets customers with a friendly "hello" when they enter the department.
4	Greets customers when they enter the department.
3	Greets customers in an unfriendly manner when they enter the department.
2	Rarely greets customers when they enter the department, and doesn't approach them to offer assistance.
1	Never greets customers when they enter the department, and doesn't approach them to offer assistance.

Appraising Performance

Learning Aid - Diagnosing Unacceptable Performance
Systemic Factors

Structure questions	Are there parts of your job that rely on other peoples' performances?
	Can you do your job when you want to, or do you have to wait for anyone else?
	Does the work come to you on time, without having to ask for it?
	Do you have to check with anybody before you can proceed with your job?
Communication questions	Do you have all the information you need to do your job?
	Is the information you need updated regularly?
	Do you get regular feedback on your performance?
	Do you have to ask for feedback on your performance?
Equipment questions	Have you got all the equipment/tools that you need to do the job?
	Can you get the equipment/tools that you require easily?
	Are the equipment/tools reliable?
	If the equipment/tools break down, are they repaired/replaced quickly?

Individual Factors

Attitude questions	Are you still enthusiastic about the job?
	Have you had any different feelings about the work recently?
	Has something changed in your personal life/work life that has affected your performance?
Skill questions	Do you feel as though you're doing the best you can?
	If your life depended on it, could you improve your performance?
	Could any sort of training help you to perform better?
Knowledge questions	The job description specifies that you need to have.... Have you got this?
	Is your knowledge up to date enough to do the job as it is now?

Learning Aid - Forced Distributions

Forced distributions can be controversial because they make someone bottom and someone top. This can feel uncomfortable and unfair if the difference between top and bottom is only marginal.

In performance appraisal, because you can assume that you have carefully selected the employee, you can significantly limit the percentage that you have to put in the bottom category.

A good model for this approach is:
- 5%-exceptional performance
- around 25 %-superior performance
- around 50%-successful performance
- around 15%-needs improvement
- 5% - unsatisfactory

Learning Aid - Self-rating Forms
Job title-Help-desk assistant
Question 1
Score yourself as follows:

5 – Well above-performance is repeatedly above expectations.

4 – Above-performance is sometimes above expectations.

3 – Meets-performance meets expectations.

2 – Below-performance is sometimes below expectations.

1 – Well below-performance is repeatedly below expectations.

- Assign a score of 1 to 5 for the following goals
- Respond to calls within the agreed on time frame
- Include new fixes in help-desk manual
- Achieve 75 percent customer satisfaction
- Make efficiency savings of 5 percent per quarter
- Attend four new software briefing sessions and make notes for coworkers

Question 2

Score yourself as follows:
3 – Improving--performance improves on previous period.
2 – Same--performance is the same as previous period.
1 – Decreasing--performance is below previous period.
Assign a score of 1 to 5 for the following performance areas
- Customer satisfaction
- Knowledge updating
- Technical solutions
- Administration
- Record keeping
-

Learning Aid - **Status Reports**
Create a form, noting the "Employee:" and the "Time period:". Then create a table with the following headings:
- Goals
- Progress: on target; ahead; behind
- Problem identification: brief details
- Check here to indicate a meeting with the manager is required to discuss the problems

CHAPTER TWO

Performance Reviews

The Performance Appraisal Discussion

If you ask managers or employees to describe the appraisal process in their organizations, they'll often describe a form-filling activity. Many organizations have become fixated on this part of the process. They measure successful appraisal by the completion rates for the paperwork.

Very often, managers enter the appraisal meeting not knowing what they're trying to achieve or how to achieve it. They often don't believe it's important. This apathy is passed onto the employee, and the appraisal becomes a pointless exercise for both of them.

Planning is essential for an effective performance appraisal discussion. You can't just appear and hope that everything will go smoothly.

An effective performance appraisal discussion needs to be comprehensively managed by the appraiser to produce an accurate, agreed on, and positive-feeling assessment of the appraisee's performance.

There are three distinct stages in an effective appraisal discussion, and a manager needs to undertake specific roles at each of these stages if the appraisal is to be successful. The first stage involves setting the scene for the discussion. The second stage covers the evaluation of the appraisee's performance, and the third stage plans for the future.

At each stage in the performance appraisal discussion, you are not only performing different roles, but you're also conducting yourself differently. You need to create a different impression each time. First, you should ensure that you're in control. Then, you should cover all aspects of the evaluation by generating a real discussion between yourself and the appraisee, which will result in an agreement. Finally, you should move from appraisal to development and put forward the best ways to support skill improvement.

Effective performance appraisal discussions

If you ask managers or employees to describe the appraisal process in their organizations, they'll often describe a form-filling activity. Many organizations have become fixated on this part of the process. They measure successful appraisal by the completion rates for the paperwork.

They've forgotten that it's the discussion that a manager and an employee have about performance, and how to improve it--not the forms--that is at the heart of the appraisal process.

Talking is an everyday occurrence in most organizations, but formal appraisal discussions are very different from casual conversations around the water cooler. There are some basic principles that must be present for a discussion to work. These are:
- Participation,
- Openness,
- Respect.

An appraisal discussion has to be managed to achieve these ends. As a manager, you're obviously in control of the appraisal process, so you determine the way that it works by your conduct. You can manage a discussion so that it is or isn't participative, open, and respectful.

Example: two different approaches for appraisal discussion.

Carl

"I'm in a hurry. I'm sure I pretty much know how you feel about your performance, so just listen to my comments first."

Rose

"Let's talk. I want to hear what you have to say. Nobody can know more about your performance than you, and I'd really value any ideas you have."

Rose encourages a dialog so that the appraisal discussion is participative, open, and respectful. She gains clear and significant benefits from this approach. She feels confident that the employee:
- has space to be honest about his opinions,
- feels safe to say what he really thinks,

- is listened to even if she disagrees with him.

Carl, however, gets through his appraisals quickly. He knows he won't have much trouble because none of his appraisees are encouraged to speak.

Effective discussions are vibrant, exciting, and challenging. That's exactly what you want from an appraisal discussion.

Characteristics of an effective performance appraisal

Very often, managers enter the appraisal meeting not knowing what they're trying to achieve or how to achieve it. They often don't believe it's important. This apathy is passed onto the employee, and the appraisal becomes a pointless exercise for both of them.

Effective performance appraisal is recognizable because it signals the point in the relationship between the manager and the employee when they come together--formally--to share their views about the previous year's performance.

An effective appraisal discussion will be a comprehensive, significant sharing of thoughts and ideas between the appraiser and appraisee. It isn't a rambling, improvised monologue by the manager. The characteristics of such a meeting are that:
- the focus is on the performance for the full year,
- the appraisal discussion is a dialog,
- there has been preparation for the discussion,
- the meeting is given importance.

Typically, an effective performance appraisal discussion will contain few surprises. Appraiser and appraisee will have exchanged rating forms so that both can be prepared. The discussion will cover all performance issues over the year.

Both sides will listen to each other and ask questions. Both parties will commit themselves to enough time to enable the discussion to be full and complete.

Example: Phil knows the true value of the appraisal discussion, and he makes sure that his appraisees also understand it. Follow along to learn how Phil opens an appraisal discussion.

> Thanks for coming. I know we've talked many times about your performance, but I think it's really important that we sit down together and review the whole year. I've got your self-rating form, and I thought we should start with you talking me through it and highlighting anything you particularly want to say.
>
> You pretty much know my view, but I was really interested in your evaluation of the design project. I still want to know why you didn't give yourself top marks. Now, I've cleared my schedule for this meeting, so let's get started. Over to you.

Each appraisal discussion is unique. It can be quite difficult to recognize the characteristics of an effective discussion when the meetings take so many forms.

Different forms that an appraisal meeting can take
    Focus

Many managers will use a "calendar" approach to the discussion. They review and discuss each month of the performance period to ensure that the focus is comprehensive.

Dialog

Asking questions--and then listening and responding to the replies--are typical, simple, and effective methods of creating a dialog. Some managers insist that the appraisee begins with a statement to ensure that there is a two-way discussion.

Preparation

Many managers will prepare for the appraisal discussion by sending a copy of their appraisal to the appraisee. This saves time and gives the appraisee an opportunity to think through what he wants to say.

Importance

Administrative acts such as advance planning, booking rooms, and allocating enough time all show the importance of the appraisal discussion. During the meeting, many managers will also reject any interruptions, which indicates the meeting's significance.

Example: appraisal discussion

Focus

Phil told his appraisee that it's really important to review performance over the whole year. He wanted to attain a fair picture of the appraisee's performance over the whole review period.

Dialog

Phil asked to hear the appraisee's own views of his performance from the self-rating form. Later, Phil asked him a direct question. Both of these techniques helped initiate a dialog.

Preparation

Phil prepared for the discussion by providing the self-rating form to his appraisee. The form contained Phil's comments, enabling the appraisee to learn Phil's views.

Importance

Phil cleared his schedule for the meeting. This clearly makes the appraisal discussion a priority for him and signals its importance.

As the appraiser, you determine whether the appraisal discussion is effective or not. If you make it focused, encourage a dialog, are prepared, and invest it with importance, it will be effective.

Stages of planning for appraisal discussions

Planning is essential for an effective performance appraisal discussion. You can't just appear and hope that everything will go smoothly.

Example: Carrie is always unprepared for appraisal discussions. Follow along as Carrie opens a discussion with Gordon.

> Carrie: Sorry I'm late. Now, you know what this is all about, don't you?
>
> Gordon: No.
>
> Carrie: Oh, it's just an appraisal discussion - nothing to worry about. I meant to tell you some time ago, but I forgot. Anyway, here are the forms we have to use. Let's read through them together and decide what we want to write.

Needless to say, Gordon was worried. He felt very angry that Carrie hadn't planned the process better. Effective appraisal discussion is the result of effective planning. There are three stages of planning that you need to consider.

Planning stages

Appraisee preparation

The first stage of planning is when you prepare the appraisee for the discussion. Here, you explain the purpose of the appraisal discussion, what will happen during it, and what the appraisee needs to do to prepare for it. This should be around a month before the discussions.

Appraiser preparation

The second stage of planning is when you prepare yourself for the discussion. Here, you complete your assessment of the appraisee and commit yourself to your final comments. This should take place around two weeks before the discussions.

Information

The third stage of planning is when you ensure that all parties have all the information they need to meaningfully take part in the discussion. This should be between a couple of days and a couple of hours before the discussions.

You don't have to strictly follow them, but these stages provide a good guideline for effective planning. They cover the significant issues of appraisee preparation, appraiser preparation, and joint preparation or information.

Example: one company integrated it into planning the appraisal discussion.

Stage 1

The company produced appraisal guidelines for appraisees, and included a brief frequently-asked-question section. All appraisers were given enough copies to distribute to their appraisees.

Stage 2

All appraisers were scheduled to meet the human resources manager for a final check two weeks before the discussions. She confirmed with all the appraisers that the paperwork had been completed and that they were confident in their judgments.

Stage 3

On the day preceding the discussion, it was company policy that all appraisees would be given a copy of the form completed by the appraisers. They could keep the form for three hours before returning it to the human resources department.

Organizations differ in the ways they go about planning for the appraisal discussion. For example, the timings suggested for each of the stages can only be indicative, although the sequence should be followed. Some organizations may prepare appraisees significantly earlier than others--one month before the discussion is only a guideline.

Planning stages

Appraisee preparation

Some organizations prepare appraisees by holding a group meeting, where the same information is imparted to them all. Many appraisers distribute the self-rating form and give the appraisees a blank copy of the appraisal form.

Appraiser preparation

One approach is to complete the assessment and put it away. It is reviewed later to double-check evidence for all the assertions. This is so that the appraiser can see it as fresh and/or share it with a coworker or manager for their comments.

Information

Many organizations give the appraisee a copy of the assessment and ask for his self-rating form. The appraiser looks for differences and identifies discrepancies. He needs to review the data and reasoning on these contentious areas.

Planning makes the appraisal discussion a far more effective process. The appraisee is prepared, you are prepared, and the information that will form the basis of the discussion is known to both parties.

Conducting an effective performance appraisal discussion

An effective performance appraisal discussion needs to be comprehensively managed by the appraiser to produce an accurate, agreed on, and positive-feeling assessment of the appraisee's performance.

There are three distinct stages in an effective appraisal discussion, and a manager needs to undertake specific roles at each of these stages if the appraisal is to be successful. The first stage involves setting the scene for the discussion. The second stage covers the evaluation of the appraisee's performance, and the third stage plans for the future.

Roles and activities that a manager must perform
Stage 1 - setting the scene

The first stage is when you explain how the meeting will run. You must take control of the meeting to make it work. Although you're creating a dialog about performance, it's on your terms- -not a free-for-all. It's important to exercise your authority now.

Stage 2 - evaluation

This is when you complete the appraisal forms. The main purpose of this stage is to create a calm dialog about performance to get the full picture. Your must balance this with helping the employee to understand and accept the final assessment of performance.

Stage 3 - the future

This stage is when you determine the response to the evaluation. Your role here is to begin the process of supporting and helping the employee improve on problem performance and maintain good performance.

Example of activities that could be performed by appraisers

Setting the scene

You could give each appraisee written guidelines about the appraisal discussion. At the start of the discussion, go over the guidelines explaining exactly how you are going to conduct the meeting.

Evaluation

You could ask the appraisee to comment on any evaluations she disagrees with. Talk through each one in turn, explaining and justifying your reasoning. Amend the ratings on the form where appropriate and ask the appraisee to initial each rating to show her agreement.

The future

You could bring a list of available training courses to the appraisal discussion. Agree on a training plan with each appraisee, which will focus on specific skills, and enroll the appraisee in the appropriate course.

Example: Rob is very clear about his role at each of the three stages of the performance appraisal discussion. Follow along to review some extracts from a recent discussion.

> I want this to be a discussion, so don't hold anything back. I've allocated an hour and I'll make sure we finish on time.
>
> I can see that you don't agree with my view on your skills as a supervisor. So, explain to me why you see it differently. I want to have your input. I'm going to coach you through your next meeting with Charlie.

Appraisers have to take on the different roles at each stage of the discussion. At stage one, Rob took on a controlling role by making it very clear that he was in charge of the meeting. But at stage two, Rob took on a role which focused more on encouraging discussion. Finally, at stage three, Rob took on the role of coach to develop the performance of the appraisee.

Activities that a manager undertakes

At each stage in the performance appraisal discussion, you are not only performing different roles, but you're also conducting yourself differently. You need to create a different impression each time. First, you should ensure that you're in control. Then, you should cover all aspects of the evaluation by generating a real discussion between yourself and the appraisee, which will result in an agreement. Finally, you should move from appraisal to development and put forward the best ways to support skill improvement.

The progression across the three stages requires a subtle change of emphasis in the way you conduct yourself.

Use the learning aid Disciplinary Checklist to remind yourself of ways to present yourself in appraisal discussions.

Setting the scene

Create control by using firm and precise statements. Confusion and loose ends will undermine the impression you want to create. Although you'll want to generate a discussion later in the appraisal, this isn't the place for it. Tell, don't ask. Insist if you have to.

Evaluation

Begin with an agreement and then move to a disagreement. Disagreements promote dialog but it will be confrontational. Agreements create a calmer dialog. Listen and respond, but ensure that you finalize the discussion to reiterate control.

The future

Development requires an enthusiastic tone to motivate the employee. You will devalue the opportunity if you are dismissive of it. You need to make employees feel that this development is specifically targeted at them, rather than being a routine response.

The style of the appraiser changes as the discussion moves through the stages. Effective appraisers tend to begin briskly before deliberately handing over to the appraisee. Then, in the final stage, they try to end on a positive and motivating note.

Example: how an appraiser adopts the appropriate style for each stage.

Setting the scene

"Right, we've only got an hour, so let's get started. I plan to give you your chance to react to my appraisal in a moment, but first, I wanted to thank you for getting your self-rating form to me on time. I considered all that you said before I decided on your evaluation."

Evaluation

"We agreed on the excellent scores for everything that required people skills. You're really good at it, aren't you? And we agreed on the below-expectations rating for the section on controlling budgets. What do you think the problem with that was?"

The future

"OK, let's sum it up. A really focused financial management program is called for.

You can see exactly why you need to do it, and I'm eager to coach you through some budget-setting techniques. We need to coordinate schedules and begin."

Case Study: Question 1 of 3

Scenario

You are appraising Scott. He's usually one of your top salespeople, but this year, he hasn't performed very well. His overall sales target has only just been met. He has rated himself as "excellent" on retaining customers but you have rated him as "below expectations." Answer the questions, in order.

Question

Scott comes into the appraisal discussion in a very upbeat mood. He has just had a call from a customer wanting to place a substantial order. He tells you that he has some good news about this quarter's target. How do you respond to him?

Options:

1. "Can we leave that? This discussion is supposed to be about last year."

2. "Maybe we can talk about that later. Perhaps it'll be relevant when we look at last year's targets."

3. "I don't know if that's relevant. I suppose we might look at it if it doesn't take up too much time."

4. "That's great news, but let's talk about it later. I want to go through your self-rating form first, and then discuss each performance area."

Answer

Actually, stage one of an appraisal discussion means that you must exercise control by using firm, brisk, and precise statements of your intentions.

Option 1: This is an incorrect option. Stage one of the appraisal discussion requires you to exercise control. By asking for Scott's opinion and permission, you've relinquished control.

Option 2: This is an incorrect option. At this stage of the appraisal discussion--stage one--you should be exercising control. This statement is full of loose ends. It lacks precision and firmness.

Option 3: This is an incorrect option. Your tone should be clear and brisk to exercise control of the appraisal discussion. This is vague and uncertain.

Option 4: This is the correct option. At stage one of an appraisal discussion, you should be exercising control. This statement is firm, brisk, and tells Scott what you intend to do.

Case Study: Question 2 of 3

Scenario

You are appraising Scott. He's usually one of your top salespeople, but this year, he hasn't performed very well. His overall sales target has only just been met. He has rated himself as "excellent" on retaining customers but you have rated him as "below expectations." Answer the questions, in order.

Question

Your instructions to Scott are that you'll begin by discussing his self-rating form. Scott says that he thinks the problem with his sales and customer retention is caused by the products. He can't see that his selling techniques are any different. How will you respond to him?

Appraising Performance

Options:

1. "I can't agree with your rating for customer retention. I scored you as 'below expectations.'"
2. "We agree on the 'acceptable' score for achieving sales targets. Why do you think you only deserved this rating this year?"
3. "So, you're saying that we haven't made the products the customers want, is that it?"
4. "I want us to concentrate on your selling techniques. That's where the real problem lies."

Answer

In fact, the second stage of an appraisal discussion is about generating and sustaining a dialog. Starting from areas of agreement and responding to the appraisee are the best techniques to do this.

Option 1: This is an incorrect option. To create a calm and controlled dialog at stage two of the appraisal discussion, it would be better to start from areas of agreement.

Option 2: This is a correct option. At stage two, you should generate a calm dialog. Starting from the areas in which you and

Scott agree is the most effective way to do this.

Option 3: This is a correct option. To sustain the dialog, you should listen and respond to Scott.

Option 4: This is an incorrect option. You aren't listening or responding to Scott. You've ignored his concerns about the products. This will not generate more discussion.

Case Study: Question 3 of 3

Scenario

You are appraising Scott. He's usually one of your top salespeople, but this year, he hasn't performed very well. His overall sales target has only just been met. He has rated himself as "excellent" on retaining customers but you have rated him as "below expectations."

Answer the questions, in order.

Question

How should you now finish the appraisal discussion?

Options:

1. "Well, I suppose some sort of product knowledge training might make a little difference."

2. "I'm absolutely sure that a product knowledge course will revitalize your sales. Just think of all the new benefits you'll be able to describe to the customers!"

3. "We're running a product knowledge course for designers next week. I know it's not quite right, but I think its best to enroll you in the next available course."

4. "The next product knowledge course isn't quite right for you. But the one after is for experienced salespeople. It's perfect for you."

Answer

In fact, the third stage of the appraisal discussion should define development opportunities. You must be enthusiastic and positive about these. You should show that the opportunity specifically focuses on the appraisee.

Option 1: This is an incorrect option. You need to enthuse and motivate Scott to develop his performance. This means you must be positive and enthusiastic--not nonchalant and disinterested.

> Option 2: This is a correct option. To energize and motivate Scott toward improvement, you must be enthusiastic and positive.
>
> Option 3: This is an incorrect option. Development opportunities should be specifically targeted at Scott to motivate him.
>
> Option 4: This is a correct option. To motivate and enthuse Scott in his development, you should ensure that you give the impression that the opportunity is specifically targeted at him.

To conduct an effective appraisal discussion with Scott, you need to control his desire to discuss his latest figures, and insist that the focus of the appraisal is on the previous year. But you also want to generate a discussion, so you should listen and respond to his views about the problems with the products.

You should begin the second stage with an area of agreement, and complete the third stage with a show of enthusiasm about the development opportunities you have devised for him. Don't leave any part of the appraisal discussion to chance. Manage each stage with subtle shifts in your behaviors and styles to conduct the most effective discussion you can.

Activity - **Planning for the Appraisal Discussion**

Think of an employee who needs a performance review. Plan when and how you will conduct the review using the following questions.

Employee Name:

Stage 1: Prepare the appraisee for the discussion

When will you meet with the employee?

How will you describe the purpose of the appraisal discussion?

How do you expect the employee to behave in the appraisal discussion?

What approach will you take to the discussion, bearing in mind how you expect the employee to react? What will you say to explain your expectations of the appraisee?

Stage 2: Prepare yourself for the discussion

When will you complete your assessment? Allow sufficient time.

Stage 3: Ensure you both have all the information you need

What information will you need for the appraisal?

What information will the appraisee need for the discussion? When will you give this information to the appraisee?

Managing Difficult Appraisals

Not all appraisees are going to respond straightforwardly to your appraisal. Appraisal, even for effective workers, can be a stressful experience. Stress typically evokes "fight or flight" responses. Anticipating and responding to these emotions is vital.

You can anticipate difficulties with employees who consistently underperform. But you still have to deal with these difficult cases with skill and professionalism.

The performance appraisal discussion is the point where you survey the worker's performance over the last year. Sometimes, this survey reveals an employee who hasn't responded to the continuous appraisal and support that has been offered to him.

Then, the nature of the performance appraisal discussion changes, and it becomes more of a disciplinary response to a consistently poor performer.

Any disciplinary response to poor performance needs to be handled by the manager with great care and precision. Many claims for unfair treatment resulting from disciplinary actions are the result of sloppy procedures. The first phase of using a disciplinary response in appraisal is when you must clearly identify the problem to the employee.

You can be sure that an appraisal meeting will evoke strong reactions in many appraisees. Even though there should be no surprises in an effective appraisal process, the actual appraisal meeting can become difficult due to the reactions of some appraisees.

Some appraisees will feel pleased, some will feel disappointed, some will be excited, and some will be subdued. Whatever their emotions, you still have to manage the appraisal process.

Managing a very emotional appraisee is going to be a challenge for every appraiser. The emotional appraisee is generally "out of control," and the appraiser needs to bring him back "under control."

Usually, the appraisee has reacted to something you have said about him. This reaction will be one of disagreement. Some appraisees may be very happy with what you say--this is unlikely to cause you problems.

The principle that underpins the first of the two components of managing the emotional appraisee - acknowledging the feelings of the appraisee--means that you must allow the appraisee to express himself, and make him feel as though you understand his feelings.

To do this requires the skill of active listening. Active listening means that you show that you've understood both the message and the feelings expressed, without necessarily agreeing with them.

Effectively managing difficult appraisals

Not all appraisees are going to respond straightforwardly to your appraisal. Appraisal, even for effective workers, can be a stressful experience. Stress typically evokes "fight or flight" responses. Anticipating and responding to these emotions is vital.

You can anticipate difficulties with employees who consistently underperform. But you still have to deal with these difficult cases with skill and professionalism.

Example: Jack wasn't anticipating any difficulties with appraising Rebecca. But he was surprised by the intensity of her feelings. He knew appraising Steve wasn't going to be easy, but Steve's reaction surprised him.

Rebecca

Rebecca yelled at Jack when he asked her to explain why she had not scored herself higher on customer service. She was really angry about her poor performance.

Steve

Steve started to cry when Jack said he had underperformed again this year. Steve was trying to manipulate Jack by making him feel sorry for him.

Jack now had to manage two distraught employees, and he really struggled to cope with them. Both reactions disconcerted him and, at first, he froze. But as Rebecca started to calm down, Jack reacted and yelled back at her. She retaliated, and he stormed out of the meeting.

Steve's tears embarrassed Jack at first, but then they disgusted him. He told Steve to stop being pathetic, and told him that he didn't deserve any bonus.

The appraisals could have been handled so much better. Jack needed skills in managing difficult appraisals.

Benefits of handling difficult appraisals

Preparation

If Jack had skills in managing difficult appraisals, he would have been prepared for the likelihood of these reactions. Then, he wouldn't have frozen. He would have anticipated the possibility of Rebecca, Steve or other employees reacting strongly to him.

Reaction

Jack's reactions were uncontrolled. Skills in managing difficult appraisals would have enabled Jack to control his emotions. Jack's reaction made the situation worse, when a controlled reaction would have calmed things down.

Responding

Jack should have responded professionally. If his original appraisal was accurate, he should not alter it because of the way Rebecca and Steve behaved. His response was petty and unjustified. He needs skills in managing difficult appraisals.

Jack was as uncontrolled as his appraisees were. Self-control is an important management quality, and vital when faced with emotional and manipulative employees. Self-control comes from preparation, and it leads to managing your own reactions to manage employees better.

Some managers reject this approach and feel that by giving free rein to their own emotions, they aren't being manipulative. But more often, they need to find an excuse for their lack of control as they emotionally dominate the employee.

The benefits of effectively managing difficult appraisals are that you are able to:
- cope with the strong emotions that you might encounter,
- control your own emotional reactions,
- respond professionally to whatever appraisees say or do.

Managing difficult appraisees requires you to stop and think before you act. This lesson will help you to think about how to react professionally to even the most difficult appraisee.

Administering a disciplinary response

The performance appraisal discussion is the point where you survey the worker's performance over the last year. Sometimes, this survey reveals an employee who hasn't responded to the continuous appraisal and support that has been offered to him.

Then, the nature of the performance appraisal discussion changes, and it becomes more of a disciplinary response to a consistently poor performer.

If you're going to consider such a serious response to a consistently poor performer, you should manage the process in two phases.

First, you must be absolutely certain that the performance problem warrants a disciplinary response.

Second, you must determine the appropriate level of that response. Before you progress with disciplinary proceedings, you must satisfy some important criteria at each of these two phases.

Criterion: Identification of the problem

There must be evidence of persistent failure to achieve the desired performance standard, and evidence of a concerted attempt to help the employee improve his performance.

Persistent failure should be defined as failure on two or more occasions.

Identification example

An employee who is always late is a typical consistently poor performer. The manager would keep records of the lateness and counsel the employee to see if any factors that are affecting punctuality could be changed.

Criterion: Assessment of the response

Any response must be in line with the company disciplinary policy. It must be comparable to previous responses to this kind of performance problem. This response should have been signaled at an earlier stage in the ongoing performance appraisal.

Assessment example

In line with most disciplinary policies, persistent lateness would warrant a warning, followed by suspension, and even dismissal. This progression would be explained to the employee from the counseling stage onwards.

Example: Here are three appraisals that involve consistently poor performers. In each case, the appraiser is considering disciplinary action against the employee.

Larry's appraisal

Larry has taken three different courses to improve his customer service skills. But complaints have still been received about him. At the last appraisal discussion, he was told that if he didn't improve, he'd be demoted in line with company policy.

Assessment of Larry's appraisal

Larry has been repeatedly warned and supported, and is aware of the consequences of his actions. The response is also in line with the company disciplinary policy, and he was aware what would happen if he didn't improve.

Stella's appraisal

Stella started to complete her work on time after the fourth warning and extensive coaching from her supervisor, but it didn't last. She knew that a coworker who hadn't met his targets was suspended in line with the company procedure.

Assessment of Stella's appraisal

Stella's performance was consistently poor. She had been supported and was aware of the consequences of her actions, which were appropriate for the offense within the company. All the criteria had been met.

Jim's appraisal

Jim had been criticized for being late with his responses to customers once before. He did it again just before his annual appraisal. His manager knew it would surprise Jim, but he felt it was justifiable to give him a written warning in line with the company policy.

Assessment of Jim's appraisal

Jim's performance is just about consistently poor. But there is no evidence that he has been supported. He hasn't been previously warned about the consequences of his actions. Not all the criteria have been met.

Criteria for a disciplinary response

Any disciplinary response to poor performance needs to be handled by the manager with great care and precision. Many claims for unfair treatment resulting from disciplinary actions are the result of sloppy procedures. The first phase of using a disciplinary response in appraisal is when you must clearly identify the problem to the employee.

Informing the employee

Define the performance gap

State clearly and unequivocally the performance problem and the occasion or occasions when it occurred by defining the performance gap. This is the difference between the performance target and the actual performance.

Identify remedial responses

State what support and help was given to the employee to try to improve his performance. State the actions taken, when they occurred, and by whom. Support is not always formal. Often, it may be informal--for example, guidance from a supervisor.

Identify worker responses

State how the employee responded to the remedial action in terms of performance. You need to be precise and acknowledge any small improvement, but compare this with the expected target. If the improvement only lasted for a short period, be sure to specify this.

Example: Chloe is appraising Alan. Follow along and note how she informs him that his performance is unsatisfactory.

> Last September, you failed to complete the end-of-month returns on time. You did the same in November and December. In September you were three days late, in November you were five days late, and in December you were ten days late.

> In September, Mary showed you a quicker way of completing the returns. This seemed to help you as you completed them on time in October. But you fell behind again in November.
>
> I then spent a couple of hours discussing prioritization of your workload with you, but you were even further behind completing the December returns. This time, you were over two weeks late.

To identify the problem with Frank, you must be very clear and precise about the performance gap and the occasions when there was evidence that he was performing below standard. You must also prove that you have offered him support--in this case, both formal and informal--and demonstrate exactly how he responded to it. Then, you have established a clear case for resorting to disciplinary action to respond to his consistently poor performance.

The second phase of handling the consistently poor performer continues from your assessment of the appropriate response to the performance. Now, you have to explain the consequences of failure to the employee, and you must be very clear and precise about how you go about this. This is a difficult time, and you'll be more effective if you're sure about your role.

There are two parts to disciplining employees.

Consequences

State the disciplinary action clearly. This will evoke a range of reactions. Don't react. Repeat your disciplinary message. If the emotional reaction persists, you should deal with it, but at this stage, try not to become sidetracked. Don't try to make the difficult news more palatable.

Confirmation

Get a written statement from the employee that states that she understands the disciplinary action. This isn't asking for her acceptance, but proof that she understands what you have said to her. Then, there can be no confusion.

Example: follow along as Chloe explains to Alan the consequences of his consistently poor performance.

Chloe: Alan, in line with our disciplinary procedure, I'm suspending you for a day for your repeated failure to complete the returns by the end of the month.

Alan: That's not fair. You can't do that.

Chloe: You'll be suspended for one day. Do you understand? Alan: Yes.

> *Chloe:* I want you to sign here to confirm that you understand that you'll be suspended for one day.

Consistently poor performers must be carefully managed. You mustn't assume that the problem is so blatant and self-evident that the response you are going to make doesn't need to be stated clearly.

Remember, even though it can seem repetitive, make sure that you have stated the performance gap. Go back over your support and make sure that the employee's response is precisely identified. Try not to respond to emotional reactions. Often, they will just go away, but if they become extreme, you'll eventually have to deal with them.

You must state the consequences of this consistently poor behavior precisely and get confirmation of his understanding. This unemotional and formal approach may seem like overkill, but these actions will protect you, and show that you have acted properly, fairly, and professionally.

Case Study: Question 1 of 2

Scenario

> Sharon has been performing poorly for the last six months. She is on the sales team, and hasn't met her targets for sufficient cold calls or for having enough customers willing to see a salesperson. She has been given support and coaching but although there have been temporary improvements, she is still below

her targets. She has been told that this level of performance only merits a lower pay scale. Use the learning aid Sharon's Appraisal Notes for information you will need to answer the questions. Answer the questions, in order.

Question

What are the first things you should say to Sharon?

Options:

1. "We both know you're not performing well enough."
2. "You were below target for cold calls for five of the last six months. For sales appointments, you were below target for four months."
3. "Whatever we've done to help you, you still don't seem to improve."
4. "I coached you in September and you took a refresher course in November."
5. "In August, there was a small improvement in your performance. But you didn't improve at all after the refresher course."

Answer

Sharon needs to be informed of the performance gap, the help she has received, and her response to it to make this an effective way of telling her that she is to be disciplined.

Option 1: This is an incorrect option. You have been too vague and imprecise. Disciplinary responses need to be precisely stated to avoid confusion and trouble later. You should emphasize the performance gap.

Option 2: This is a correct option. You have made a statement that is clear and precise. You have identified the performance gap, which signals the performance problem.

Option 3: This is an incorrect option. You haven't acknowledged that Sharon made a small improvement in August.

Option 4: This is a correct option. You have noted both the formal and the informal support given to Sharon.

Option 5: This is a correct option. Even though the general pattern is poor, you have clearly indicated even the small improvement in August.

Case Study: Question 2 of 2
Scenario

Sharon has been performing poorly for the last six months. She is on the sales team, and hasn't met her targets for sufficient cold calls or for having enough customers willing to see a salesperson. She has been given support and coaching but although there have been temporary improvements, she is still below her targets. She has been told that this level of performance only merits a lower pay scale. Use the learning aid [Sharon's Appraisal Notes](#) for information you will need to answer the questions. Answer the questions, in order.

Question

Sharon isn't surprised when you tell her that she'll be put on a lower pay scale, but she doesn't accept that the below-target performance is her fault. She tells you that the other sales team members can't make the required number of calls per day either. How do you respond to this comment?

Options:

1. "That's not the issue. I'm here to discuss your performance. I haven't heard that anybody else is performing as poorly as you. Where's your evidence?"

2. "As a result of your consistently poor performance, you'll be put on the lower pay scale immediately." 3. "I want you to sign this form to show that you agree with the disciplinary action."

4. "I want you to sign this form to show that you understand the terms of the disciplinary action."

Answer

Actually, you should restate the disciplinary action and refuse to respond to Sharon's comments. Then, you need to get proof that she has understood the action you are taking.

Option 1: This is an incorrect option. You shouldn't allow yourself to be sidetracked by Sharon's comments. Your role here is to restate the disciplinary action, not debate it.

Option 2: This is a correct option. You shouldn't respond to Sharon's comments, but simply restate the disciplinary action that you intend to take.

Option 3: This is an incorrect option. By asking Sharon to sign the form, your intention is to have proof that she has understood the disciplinary action, not to get her to agree with it.

Option 4: This is a correct option. By asking Sharon to sign the form, your intention is to have proof that she has understood the disciplinary action.

When disciplining her, the opening statement should be about Sharon's poor performance. The performance gap between her efforts and the required standard is the best vehicle for this. But you must also show how you have tried to help her and how she has responded.

Then, you are in the right position to proceed and explain the detail of your disciplinary action, and ensure that she acknowledges that she has heard correctly what you have said to her.

Disciplining one of your team members for consistently poor performance isn't easy. But you should make sure that you have acted efficiently, effectively, and professionally so that both you and the employee can move on from this point.

Types of difficult appraisees

You can be sure that an appraisal meeting will evoke strong reactions in many appraisees. Even though there should be no surprises in an effective appraisal process, the actual appraisal meeting can become difficult due to the reactions of some appraisees.

Some appraisees will feel pleased, some will feel disappointed, some will be excited, and some will be subdued. Whatever their emotions, you still have to manage the appraisal process.

A typical response to appraisal will include some understandably heightened emotions. But some appraisees will go beyond this. They will exhibit an extreme and very difficult reaction. You're likely to come across two main types of appraisees who react in such extreme ways.

Extreme reactions during an appraisal

The angry appraisee

These are people whose behaviors can range from an uncontrolled loss of temper, to rage. They might yell at you, and even threaten abuse and violence.

The distraught appraisee

These are people who are very depressed by the appraisal. Typically, their responses might range from persistent crying, to hysterical weeping.

If an angry appraisee yells, it is a conventional--albeit extreme--reaction. Sometimes, however, appraisees' responses are far more complex, and recognizing whether they are just angry responses is difficult.

Complexity of responses

Anger at themselves

Appraisees will accept and own responsibility for poor performances. Their anger is with themselves because they have been incompetent. They may say that they have disappointed the team. These appraisees may feel ashamed. Apologies will be continuous, extreme, and vehement.

Anger with everybody else

Appraisees have transferred the responsibility for their poor performances onto others. The problem is a lack of support or resources-- never themselves. They won't accept any rational arguments about their behaviors.

They won't appear to be angry, but will repeat their justifications.

Angry appraisees can exhibit basic responses or responses that are far more complex to decipher.

Example: two different types of angry reactions to appraisal. Harry and Jessica are showing basic anger. But Milly and Belle's angry reactions are far more complex.

Harry

Harry was so angry when his appraiser told him that he wasn't getting a bonus, that he couldn't sit down any longer. Once on his feet, he started waving his arms about and yelling. He banged on the desk as he tried to make his point.

Jessica

Jessica just sat there for a moment when she was told about the demotion. Then, she swept everything off the desk, tore the appraisal form into pieces, and threw them at the appraiser. She stormed out, slamming the door so hard that the glass broke.

Milly

Milly was ashamed that she had failed to hit her targets. She'd disappointed the whole team. She was so angry with herself that she vowed to work every weekend until she exceeded her goal. She apologized time and time again.

Belle

Belle said that it wasn't her fault. The rest of the team had sabotaged her work and made it impossible for her to keep up to date. She wouldn't discuss anything else. She just repeated her assertion that the rest of the team was making her look incompetent.

Distraught appraisees can also show basic and complex reactions. A basic reaction is typically crying, but complex reactions may be far more subtle.

Different reactions

Extreme shock

Typically, these appraisees have ignored all previous warnings. They are in denial about their problems. The appraisal means that they can no longer ignore the process. They respond by freezing, and are incapable of speech or action. These appraisees are extremely distraught, but emotionally numb.

Extreme upset

These appraisees react tearfully as a manipulative device. They hope to embarrass the appraiser to encourage leniency. The emotions they express are shallow and they aren't genuine.

Here are some examples of appraisees who exhibit extreme reactions to appraisals. Neil and Julie show conventional basic distraught reactions. Eric and Don's reactions are far more subtle.

Neil

Neil broke down in tears during his appraisal. He apologized and the meeting halted while he composed himself. But every time the appraiser tried to start again, Neil began sobbing. After an hour, the meeting was canceled.

Julie

Julie shrieked in horror when she heard she wasn't getting her bonus. She completely broke down and her sobs could be heard all over the office. People came out to see what the matter was, but she couldn't stop. She just got louder and louder.

Eric

Eric didn't reply when his manager told him he was being demoted. He just stared out of the window. His manager tried to help him communicate, but Eric just sat there.

Eventually, his manager gave up and left Eric on his own for a while.

Don

Don started to sob after Claire told him he was to be suspended. Claire was embarrassed and looked away. Don noted her reaction and cried even harder. When she went to get him a drink of water, he thought he was winning.

The extreme responses that appraisees can exhibit are a challenge. If you can understand why appraisees are reacting in the ways they are, you'll have a much better chance of dealing with them.

Managing the emotional appraisee

Managing a very emotional appraisee is going to be a challenge for every appraiser. The emotional appraisee is generally "out of control," and the appraiser needs to bring him back "under control."

Usually, the appraisee has reacted to something you have said about him. This reaction will be one of disagreement. Some appraisees may be very happy with what you say--this is unlikely to cause you problems.

Your task is to deal with the emotions as quickly as possible and continue with the appraisals. Therefore, there are two components that you have to consider to be successful at managing the emotional appraisee. You must deal with both the appraisee's emotional reactions and your original statement that provoked the response.

Acknowledge emotions

Ignoring emotions is counterproductive, as is reacting in kind to them. Both will increase, rather then defuse, the emotional temperature. You must keep your self-control.

Acknowledge and work through the emotions to move on.

Maintain your position

Unless you have made a thoughtless remark, the statement that provoked the response is an important part of your appraisal. So, you must hold to it--don't apologize. Although it's preferable for the appraisee to eventually agree with you, it's not essential.

It's difficult to be in control of yourself when others have lost their self-control. But if you hold onto the job you should be doing--appraising the employee's performance--then it can be easier.

How to behave when faced with an angry appraisee
Acknowledge

When the appraisee starts yelling, you shouldn't yell back or back down. You should calmly acknowledge that the appraisee is feeling angry.

Make your statement

You should then remind the appraisee that you have the right to conduct the appraisal. Make your statement again, and try to move on.

Dealing with an appraisee who had lost control

Brad

Brad's appraisal of Clancy started to go wrong when Clancy started yelling. Brad ignored Clancy and carried on. Clancy got more and more angry, and eventually stormed out of the room.

Jim

Jim wasn't going to back down when Steve started yelling--he yelled back. When an employee from the office next door came in to see what the noise was about, the two of them were pushing each other around.

Alice

Alice desperately wanted Milly to agree with her. Alice tried everything to persuade her.

The appraisal started to flounder as Alice went back over the same ground. Milly wouldn't agree with her, but Alice wouldn't stop trying.

Cory

Cory noted the conviction in Keysha's voice. Maybe he was wrong--Keysha seemed so sure about it. He still wasn't convinced that she was right, but perhaps he should reconsider some of his assessments. He struggled on.

Brad didn't acknowledge Clancy's feelings and Jim didn't control his own feelings. Alice was too focused on getting Milly to agree with her and Cory backed down. None of these appraisals really worked.

By acknowledging feelings and sticking to their assessments, managers can be successful at handling emotional appraisees. Megan, Charles, Clyde, and Cynthia did.

Megan

Megan listened carefully as Frank started to get angry. She acknowledged that he didn't agree with her and that she could understand his feelings. Frank calmed down a little and they agreed to differ.

Charles

Charles could feel his temper rising as Leonie vehemently refused to accept his comments. She got angrier and angrier. Charles took some deep breaths and got his emotions under control. Then, he concentrated on what Leonie was saying.

Clyde

Clyde was surprised by the strength of Darren's reaction. Darren was adamant that Clyde was wrong. Clyde checked his notes and repeated his statements. He was sure he was right, and he wasn't going to back down now.

Cynthia

Cynthia was sure that Paul wouldn't agree with her rating. She talked it through and tried to get Paul to see her point of view, but he wouldn't, so she moved on. She'd made her point and needed to make plenty of other comments.

Megan dealt with Frank's anger and Charles controlled his own temper. Clyde stuck to his original statement and Cynthia accepted that Paul didn't agree with her.

These four managers managed the appraisal process well. They acknowledged their appraisees' feelings -

which included putting aside their own feelings--and reiterated their statements before moving on.

Principles of managing the emotional appraisee

The principle that underpins the first of the two components of managing the emotional appraisee - acknowledging the feelings of the appraisee--means that you must allow the appraisee to express himself, and make him feel as though you understand his feelings.

To do this requires the skill of active listening. Active listening means that you show that you've understood both the message and the feelings expressed, without necessarily agreeing with them.

Active listening encompasses all of the usual listening skills. But it also includes paraphrasing your understanding of the employee's message and the feelings that come with it. You are proving that you're really listening. This will often defuse the emotion.

Paraphrasing the message and the feelings

The message

Simply and briefly restate the main issues in the appraisee's message. You shouldn't interpret or comment on this message. You're showing that you have understood.

The feelings

Describe your assessment of the feelings that come with the message. You're empathizing, not criticizing or condoning these feelings.

When an appraisee starts crying, it's difficult to remain unemotional. The best way to do this is to make a comment like, "I can see that being rated below expectations for efficiency upsets you." This shows that you've listened. Then you should say something that shows how you understand these emotions--

to check with the appraisee that your interpretation is correct. A statement like, "You're upset because you think you're as efficient as the other team members," would work in this situation.

Remember that you are showing active listening skills. Appraisees who feel that someone has listened to their points of view may well be satisfied and calm down. But even if they are not, you can be assured that you are handling the situation in the best way possible.

Example: Chelsea is very angry that Melissa has rated her as "below expectations" on punctuality. Follow along as Melissa actively listens to Chelsea.

> **Chelsea:** It's not right. You know I've had car trouble. I couldn't help being late sometimes. You've never liked me. You wouldn't treat anybody else like this.
>
> **Melissa:** OK, you think I'm singling you out for poor punctuality. You're angry because you don't think it's fair.
>
> **Chelsea:** Yes, that's right.

Melissa listens to both the message and the feelings behind it. She shows that she understands exactly what Chelsea is saying by paraphrasing. Chelsea responds by starting to calm down.

But Melissa still has to continue with the appraisal. Her judgment is that Chelsea isn't punctual and she must stick to this assessment. This is the second part of managing emotional appraisees. You must ensure that the original assessment is reiterated. The best way to do this is to construct a three-part message. The message must cover purpose, evidence, and repetition.

The three-part message

Purpose

Begin by reminding the appraisee of the purpose of the meeting and your role as manager--to objectively assess the performance of the employees. In this way, you're putting your authority into context. Don't apologize for your decision.

Evidence

Remind the appraisee of your evidence. You're showing him that your decision is objective and justified. The evidence that you've used must be clear and specific, and relate precisely to your assessment.

Repeat

Repeat your assessment. You need to show that you have not changed it in light of the emotional reaction. But you should acknowledge the feelings that have been created. You're making the final definitive assessment, which will not change.

Now, Melissa has to continue and reiterate the original assessment that provoked Chelsea's anger.

"As your manager, it's my job to complete your appraisal. Last quarter, you were late on five occasions. Three of those times you didn't come in until after lunch. No other employee has been late more than once. I recognize that you're angry because you think it's not fair. But my assessment stands. You are "below expectations" on punctuality."

Melissa's calm, methodical, and justified assessment--coupled with her active listening--will defuse Chelsea's emotions and allow the appraisal to continue.

Case Study: Question 1 of 2

Scenario

You are appraising Erin. When you tell her that her performance in teamwork is unsatisfactory, she angrily disagrees. Your assessment is based on the monthly team meetings that you have convened. Erin is rarely prepared for these meetings, and has frequently failed to complete her part of the tasks assigned to her team. She always blames the other team members, and her relationship with her coworkers has completely deteriorated.

Answer the questions, in order.

Question

Erin angrily tells you that you are siding with her coworkers. She thinks that you've deliberately assigned her the most difficult tasks, and because her coworkers have been uncooperative, she has failed through no fault of her own. How should you respond to these remarks?

Options:

1. "You expect me to believe that all of the rest of your team have sabotaged your performance?"
2. "You think that your performance has been affected because your tasks were more difficult than the rest of the team. And because your coworkers wouldn't assist you as they should."
3. "You're just trying to be the victim by making it look as though I don't like you."
4. "You feel that I have deliberately been unfair in allocating work to you."

Answer

In fact, you should have shown that you have actively listened to Erin by restating both her comments, and the feelings that surround them. This is the most effective way of defusing such an emotional reaction.

Option 1: This is an incorrect option. In this approach you make a comment about Erin's statement. This will not defuse the emotion; it will increase it. A neutral reiteration of her statement is the best way to handle this.

Option 2: This is a correct option. You have simply restated Erin's remark. This shows active listening and will, in part, help to defuse the emotional reaction.

Option 3: This is an incorrect option. You should not try to interpret Erin's comments.

Option 4: This is a correct option. By restating Erin's feelings back to her, you have shown that you have actively listened to her. This is the most effective way of defusing emotional reactions quickly.

Case Study: Question 2 of 2
Scenario

You are appraising Erin. When you tell her that her performance in teamwork is unsatisfactory, she angrily disagrees. Your assessment is based on the monthly team meetings that you have convened. Erin is rarely prepared for these meetings, and has frequently failed to complete her part of the tasks assigned to her team. She always blames the other team members, and her relationship with her coworkers has completely deteriorated.

Answer the questions, in order.

Question

After your response Erin calms down a little, but she still insists that the tasks she was given were more difficult than the ones given to the rest of her team. She also still asserts that if her coworkers had been more cooperative with her, then she would have completed her tasks on time. How should you respond to her this time?

Options:

1. "I'm sorry, Erin, but I don't think you have been an effective team worker."
2. "Erin, as your manager, it's my job to assess your performance. You have failed to complete your part
of a team task on four occasions."
3. "Erin, we both know you haven't played your part in some team tasks."

4. "Erin, my assessment is that you have been unsatisfactory as a team worker."

5. "Erin, in light of your reaction, I'm willing to alter my assessment to say that you are a satisfactory team worker."

Answer

Actually, you should close the discussion on the issue by expressing your authority and the purpose of the meeting. Then by citing clear evidence and restating your assessment, you can move on.

Option 1: This is an incorrect option. By apologizing, you devalue your authority. This is likely to make Erin feel that if she continues her protest, she may make you change your assessment.

Option 2: This is a correct option. You have put the situation in context and justified your authority to make this assessment. You have also provided evidence for your assertion. This will enable you to bring closure to this episode and move on.

Option 3: This is an incorrect option. Your evidence is too vague and uncertain. This will more than likely provoke Erin to debate the matter further when you are trying to move on.

Option 4: This is a correct option. This simple restatement of your assessment--without any change-- should bring closure to the issue and enable you to move on.

Option 5: This is an incorrect option. If you indicate that you are willing to consider changing your assessment, you will naturally provoke further debate. If your original assessment was correct, you should stick to it and move on.

Erin's emotional reaction is best handled by a combination of active listening and firmly restating the assessment that provoked the response.

Appraisees who react emotionally can easily sidetrack the meeting. You need to respect their feelings by active listening, but you then need to firmly bring closure to the episode and move on with the appraisal.

Developing Better Performance

One of the fundamental goals of appraisal is to develop better performance. This aspect of appraisal often gets lost when both appraisers and appraisees concentrate too much upon the assessment of past performance, and become focused on performance ratings to the exclusion of everything else.

All employees can probably improve their performances if they work harder, faster or more efficiently. But a manager also needs to play an important role in helping the employee to improve by creating the opportunities that help to improve performance.

Time and money will probably limit any attempt to create new and specific development opportunities. One of the best ways to develop an employee is to involve him in some naturally occurring activities.

After you've identified a challenging opportunity, you must then determine which employees would best benefit from the opportunity. Challenging projects that are large-scale, complex, and highly interactive provide opportunities for employees to develop interpersonal skills in leadership (leading and managing others), relationship-building (working with unfamiliar people), and influencing (persuading people).

When an employee is faced with the challenge of developing or improving his skills as a result of being appraised, the manager has to take an active role in supporting the employee.

The manager must not only create opportunities for the employee to develop skills, but also actively coach and motivate the employee in the demanding struggle for continual development and improvement. These two interventions--coaching and motivating--can often make the difference between the employee who grabs hold of the development opportunities, and the employee who cannot.

Coaching is appropriate for employees who can't seem to learn the new skills that they need in order to perform better. They are aware that there is a problem, but can't resolve it. They tend to perform in the same old unsatisfactory ways, even though they know this is ineffective. This often creates frustration. When you coach them, be aware that your nondirective approach may easily get an angry response.

For some managers, any sort of training equals development. They think that their responsibility for supporting the development of employees is fulfilled by sending them on the next available training course.

But they are wrong. Training is a useful part of developing an employee if it is specifically designed to help that employee improve performance.

Supporting employees to improve performance

One of the fundamental goals of appraisal is to develop better performance. This aspect of appraisal often gets lost when both appraisers and appraisees concentrate too much upon the assessment of past performance, and become focused on performance ratings to the exclusion of everything else.

Because of this emphasis on assessment and ratings--as opposed to development--many appraisees feel that appraisal is a process done to them, not with them.

To address this problem, you need to show that effective appraisal involves both appraiser and appraisee. The development of better performance provides an ideal opportunity to show a change of "ownership," because it involves more self-responsibility, self-motivation, and partnership. As the appraiser, you need to act more as a facilitator.

self-responsibility

Place the responsibility for constant improvement on the employee. Do this by defining your task as one of creating the best performance conditions that will encourage and support the employee to excel. Your expectations are the key to encouraging self-responsibility.

self-motivation

You can only motivate employees so far. Real motivation comes from within. So, your role isn't just to encourage the employee to perform better, but to help him to find the keys to his self- motivation. Support and encourage him as well as you can to perform better and better.

partnership

You have power, control, and authority as a manager, but the employee has responsibility and motivation. By combining these forces in a partnership, effective development takes place. You have to be a facilitator as well as a manager.

This lesson will show you how to establish the best conditions to improve performance, define development activities with the appraisee, and determine some effective training interventions. The benefits of this facilitative approach are that you:
- increase self-responsibility in appraisees
- encourage self-motivation for constant improvement
- develop a partnership approach with appraisees over development issues.

Self-responsibility, self-motivation, and partnership do not just happen. They are the products of appraisers choosing to act deliberately to increase these forces. Inevitably, this involves the appraiser taking a step back and giving the appraisee more scope. Some managers struggle when moving toward a facilitation role. They feel that it is a loss of authority. But often, what they are really saying is that they don't trust their employees.

Example of a manager who has been able to facilitate as well as to control in an appraisal.

Self-responsibility

Carlos asks employees what new skills they want to develop, and then they devise a new assignment together that will challenge the employees to develop these skills. Employees can choose not to accept the assignment, or can modify it if they wish.

Self-motivation

Mary's team motto is, "pride in all we do." Mary gives team members regular feedback to help them evaluate their own performances. The team members vote each month to select the employee who has tried the hardest, and that worker is given a small prize.

Partnership

Scott runs a skills workshop each month. Employees can attend if they want to, and Scott will focus on one aspect of their skills. Someone suggested he should make the classes compulsory but Scott refused. He feels the voluntary aspect is vital to its success.

Better performance results from a partnership between appraiser and appraisee. The appraiser should facilitate an increase in self-responsibility and self-motivation. This is what produces performance improvement.

Creating the best performance opportunities

All employees can probably improve their performances if they work harder, faster or more efficiently. But a manager also needs to play an important role in helping the employee to improve by creating the opportunities that help to improve performance.

Time and money will probably limit any attempt to create new and specific development opportunities. One of the best ways to develop an employee is to involve him in some naturally occurring activities.

The best activities for development are likely to be specific projects that occur naturally. You can then place the employee inside the project to improve the particular skills that need developing. The best projects for developing your employees will have one overriding characteristic--they will be a challenge. To be a challenge, the projects mustn't be easy for the employee, and must require the employee to work in new and demanding ways.

Such projects are not everyday occurrences, but when they do come along, you must first recognize that they are a development opportunity. Then, you must use them to develop particular skills in particular employees.

The first thing you need to do is recognize what sorts of projects would be usable as challenging development opportunities. It's easy to be vague and define every project as a challenge. There are, however, some more specific characteristics that you can look for.

A good development opportunity

> **Scale**
>
> The scale of the project obviously influences the extent of the challenge. Projects that involve large numbers of people--even if only in a passive role, such as organizing a conference-- demand considerable organizing skills.
>
> **Complexity**

Complexity follows from scale. Complexity implies a multi-faceted project so that a range of activities, events or people have to be brought together efficiently and seamlessly to a single point.

Interaction

Interaction means the variety of people involved in the project. External entities are very demanding of skills in interaction. Competing vested interests in a project increase the challenge. Planned events involve much more detailed interaction than unplanned events.

Here are some typical projects. They show some of the characteristics of challenge that are necessary in development opportunities.

Project can be an appropriate vehicle for developing employees.

off-site conference

This sort of event is difficult to organize. Using off-site accommodations is likely to involve extensive interaction with external entities. The conference will require the coordination of a complicated timetable if it involves guest speakers.

companywide briefing

A briefing involving the whole company is likely to involve a series of large-scale meetings. Such meetings require considerable interaction with all parts of the company. Maintaining productivity and running such a briefing is a highly complex task.

visit of a very important person (VIP) and entourage

A very important person (VIP) and associated entourage don't just appear. There will be advance negotiations, and management of the agreed on schedule with in-house employees. This is very complex and likely to require great interaction skills.

launch of a new product

The launch of a new product is the culmination of a lot of effort and investment. There are probably numerous vested interests, which will need to be reconciled. Many parts of the project will need to be assembled by launch day. The scale of financial loss from a poor launch will be considerable.

Now you need to arrange some of the attributes of the project so that they will best develop the skills of your employees. You can do this by putting an employee in a certain role within the project and by managing some of the details of the project. Then, you can create the best possible performance conditions for a specific employee to develop a specific skill.

Laverne and Trudi are managers who have used projects as opportunities to challenge some of their employees to develop and improve their skills.

Example: more about the scale, complexity, and interaction in the projects they have used.

Laverne

Laverne used the organization and dissemination of a cross-company newsletter as an ideal project. This involved finding and editing news items from every department.

Trudi

Trudi's project was moving human resources support from a main office to every site. The project team had to decide on every aspect of the plan.

Characteristics of challenging development projects

After you've identified a challenging opportunity, you must then determine which employees would best benefit from the opportunity. Challenging projects that are large-scale, complex, and highly interactive provide opportunities for employees to develop interpersonal skills in leadership (leading and managing others), relationship-building (working with unfamiliar people), and influencing (persuading people).

Skillgroups

Leadership skills

You're likely to want to develop leadership skills in employees who are technically proficient but lack the drive and assertiveness to take control of coworkers. Although they may know what to do, they'll always take less responsibility and let others lead.

Relationship-building skills

Relationship-building skills are needed by those who find it difficult to work in new situations with unfamiliar people. These employees are too reticent and shy. They'll avoid situations in which they have to work with strangers.

Influencing skills

Employees who need influencing skills typically tend to use their positions or technical expertise to overpower coworkers. They don't listen to other points of view. They don't persuade--they insist that things be done their way.

Example: Dean, Rick, Molly, Simon, Grace, and Phil have some problems with leadership, relationship-building, and influencing skills. Karen, their manager, has made her assessment of their problems.

Dean

"He's the best qualified and most experienced person on the team. But he lacks leadership skills. When there's a problem, no one looks to him for the solution and he doesn't push himself forward. He lets pushy coworkers lead the team in the wrong direction because he won't say anything."

Rick

"Rick lacks influencing skills. He knows what he's talking about. He's got all of the certificates. But he doesn't listen to the people who don't know as much as he does. He tells them exactly what to do, and he expects them to do it."

Molly

"Molly is shy - she always has been, so building relationships is hard for her. But since she took on this new job, it's become a real issue. I'm sure some of the customers visiting the exhibitions think she's a fool, or just not interested in them. She finds it hard to go up and just start talking to people."

Simon

"Simon lacks relationship-building skills. He's anxious that new people won't think he knows what he's doing. So he makes sure his contributions are noticed. He just can't stop talking sometimes."

Grace

"Grace needs to develop some influencing skills. People think she talks too much, and she's really loud. I can see the look on their faces. But she does know what she's talking about and she's usually right. But her coworkers complain that she's too 'bossy.' They certainly don't want to work with her."

Phil

"Phil lacks leadership. He just lets people get on with making their mistakes. He thinks they're 'foolish.' If they asked him, he could tell them what to do. But they don't, so he just gets on with his own work."

Recommended actions for major skill groups

Leadership - recommended action

Put the employee in a clear and obvious leadership role. Emphasize the need for dynamic leadership skills by ensuring that the assignment has a testing and demanding time scale. Avoid any form of solo work. This employee needs to lead a team.

Leadership - example
Responsibility for planning an executive's visit is an ideal development opportunity. It will involve leading a team, which includes the executive's representatives. This planning will need to be completed before any other arrangements are made.

Relationship-building - recommended action
Give this employee tasks that require him to initiate and sustain contact with unfamiliar people. Avoid solo work situations unless they include lots of contact with others. Choose team situations, unless they are competitive.

Relationship-building - example
In a project to set up a new branch office, the task of contacting realtors to view prospective sites is an excellent relationship-building opportunity.

Influencing - recommended action
Put the employee on a team in which she has no positional power, and her coworkers are equal. Avoid solo work unless it involves persuading others. On a team, this employee

must influence, not insist. This will encourage compromise.

Influencing - example

Negotiating with senior managers to organize and confirm their attendance at a series of cross- company seminars will be a good and challenging opportunity for an employee who needs to develop influencing skills.

Phil was in overall charge of a project to arrange a very prestigious off-site conference with some internationally renowned guest speakers. Using employees from across the company, he set up teams to contact the guest speakers and agree on a timetable. This had to be finalized quickly to confirm all of the other arrangements. Another team had to agree on which in-house employees would speak at the conference. This was a contentious issue. Each department wanted to be represented with a good time slot for its speaker.

Phil also identified some individual tasks that needed to be completed. One was contacting hotels to find the best accommodations for the conference. Another was to contact and persuade some significant shareholders to attend the conference.

Phil wanted to use the conference to develop the skills of some employees. Shannon needed to develop her leadership skills, Martin was very shy, and Nicole used her status to ignore the opinions of her coworkers.

Phil allocated roles in the project to each employee according to the development need.

What employees did and why

Shannon
Shannon was to lead the team contacting the guest speakers. Being officially in charge of a team would help her to develop her leadership skills. A deadline would help her to become a dynamic and assertive leader. Giving her an individual task wouldn't have helped her to improve her leadership skills.

Martin
Martin was to be given a role that involved contacting other people. He would be on the team that contacted guest speakers, and his individual task could be either contacting hotels or shareholders. This would help him to develop relationship-building skills.

Nicole
Nicole was to be put on the team that decided on the in-house contributors. She was of equal status so she would be forced to use influencing and persuading skills, rather than power. Her individual task was to contact shareholders. This would require persuasion skills.

Case Study: Question 1 of 3
Scenario

You want to improve the performance of some employees in your company. Greg is a senior member of the design team. Tara is the administrative assistant in the human resources department, and Alicia is the assistant team leader in the marketing department. There is quite a big project coming up to produce the annual in-house magazine, known as "The Broadcast." Use the learning aid Annual Broadcast Project for information you will need to answer the questions.

Answer the questions, in order.

Question

How would you use the project--to publish the in-house magazine--to create the best performance opportunity for Greg?

Options:

1. I wouldn't allow Greg to work individually.
2. I'd make Greg a member of the team that deals with external advertising.
3. I'd make Greg the person who has to arrange for each department head to write an article.

4. I'd put Greg in charge of the team that organizes the "Employee of the Year" award.
Answer
In fact, Greg needs to develop his leadership skills. He will benefit most from being made a leader of a team with a tight deadline.

Option 1: This is a correct option. Greg needs to develop leadership skills. Any individual work, of whatever nature, will not help him to develop these skills.

Option 2: This is an incorrect option. Greg needs to lead a team to develop his leadership skills. Being a team member will not help him in this respect.

Option 3: This is an incorrect option. This is an individual task. An individual task means that Greg will not lead anybody, so this won't help him to develop his leadership skills.

Option 4: This is a correct option. Greg is likely to develop leadership skills if he is made the formal leader of a group. If there are tight deadlines, as in this case, this will help him to be more dynamic and assertive.

Case Study: Question 2 of 3
Scenario

You want to improve the performance of some employees in your company. Greg is a senior member of the design team. Tara is the administrative assistant in the human resources department, and Alicia is the assistant team leader in the marketing department. There is quite a big project coming up to produce the annual in-house magazine, known as "The Broadcast." Use the learning aid Annual Broadcast Project for information you will need to answer the questions.

Answer the questions, in order.

Question

How would you use the project to help Tara develop the interpersonal skills that she has problems with?

Options:

1. I'd make Tara a member of the team that has to agree on the layout of The Broadcast.
2. I'd give Tara the personal task of contacting department heads to arrange for them to write an article for The Broadcast.
3. I'd make Tara a member of the team tasked with arranging external advertising. 4. I

would ask Tara to do the accounting for The Broadcast.

Answer

Actually, Tara needs to develop her relationship-building skills. She would benefit from being involved with a team that makes external contacts. Her individual task should be one that involves lots of interaction with others.

Option 1: This is an incorrect option. Tara is shy. Such a competitive environment would not suit her. It would be more likely to increase her shyness, rather than encourage her to develop relationships with people.

Option 2: This is a correct option. This individual task involves a great deal of contact with others. It would help Tara to develop her relationship-building skills.

Option 3: This is a correct option. As a team member of a group needing to contact external parties, Tara would be encouraged to develop her relationship-building skills.

Option 4: This is an incorrect option. This is an individual task with little or no interaction with others. This would not help Tara with her relationship-building skills.

Case Study: Question 3 of 3
Scenario

You want to improve the performance of some employees in your company. Greg is a senior member of the design team. Tara is the administrative assistant in the human resources department, and Alicia is the assistant team leader in the marketing department. There is quite a big project coming up to produce the annual in-house magazine, known as "The Broadcast." Use the learning aid Annual Broadcast Project for information you will need to answer the questions.

Answer the questions, in order.

Question

How would you allocate a role to Alicia in the project to create the best development opportunities for her?

Options:

1. Alicia should be a member of the team that has to agree on the layout of The Broadcast.

2. Alicia should lead the team that has to agree on the layout of The Broadcast.
3. Alicia should do the accounting for The Broadcast.
4. Alicia should have the individual task of getting senior executives to donate a prize for the crossword competition in the magazine.

Answer

In fact, Alicia needs to develop her influencing skills. She will benefit from team situations in which she is of equal status with the other team members. Her individual task should focus on persuading others.

Option 1: This is a correct option. Alicia needs to learn how to influence people. On a team like this where she would have equal status with others, she would have a good chance to develop those skills.

Option 2: This is an incorrect option. Alicia uses her positional power to ignore people. Any role as a leader of a team would encourage that behavior. She needs to be on a team where she is of equal status with others.

Option 3: This is an incorrect option. Alicia should only be given an individual task that requires a lot of persuading of other people. This task does not fulfill that requirement.

Option 4: This is a correct option. Alicia needs to develop skills in persuading rather then overwhelming other people. This task is perfectly suited to develop this skill.

Making Greg lead a team with a tight deadline will help him to develop his leadership skills. But individual work would only encourage his tendency to work on his own. Tara can be helped if she is given roles, both as a team member and individually, that involve lots of contact with unfamiliar people.

Alicia needs to be in roles in which she can't use status or expertise to ignore others' inputs. Working on the competitive Broadcast layout team and a role trying to persuade senior executives will develop her influencing skills.

Using available projects for targeted development is a highly efficient and effective way to create the best performance opportunities.

Developing employees

When an employee is faced with the challenge of developing or improving his skills as a result of being appraised, the manager has to take an active role in supporting the employee.

The manager must not only create opportunities for the employee to develop skills, but also actively coach and motivate the employee in the demanding struggle for continual development and improvement. These two interventions--coaching and motivating--can often make the difference between the employee who grabs hold of the development opportunities, and the employee who cannot.

Characteristics of effective coaching and motivating

Coaching

A coach acts as a supportive sounding board to help employees through a learning experience. A coach is not directive. A coach doesn't tell employees how to act, but encourages them to reflect on their actions. Coaches do not blame.

Example of coaching

In a situation where an employee is having difficulty dealing with aggressive customers, a coach won't tell the employee what to do. The coach will prompt the employee to reflect on ways she might handle more aggressive customers.

Motivating

A motivator supports employees by encouraging them through difficult periods. This is not careless, random encouragement but calculated and honest support in the form of feedback to employees on the progress in their work.

Example of motivating

An employee who feels that she is performing poorly can be reminded that in the previous performance period, she was well ahead of her targets. General encouragement lacks this precise feedback.

Here is how a manager should and should not act as a coach and a motivator. In this situation, the employee, Dean, is trying to develop a more assertive approach to his relationships with coworkers. He is finding it very difficult.

Example: how Katy can be an effective coach and motivator.

Effective coaching

Katy asks Dean to talk her through the last time he consciously tried to be more assertive. She asks him to replay the conversation and identify what he thought went wrong.

Effective motivating

Katy reminds him of the times he has been successful in asserting himself. She contrasts his assertive behavior now with how it used to be.

Ineffective coaching

Katy instructs Dean in the techniques that will make him more assertive. She describes how he behaved, and criticizes his performance.

Ineffective motivating

Katy pats Dean on the back and tells him that he is doing a great job. She tells him that she has never seen anyone develop assertiveness skills as quickly and effectively.

Coaching and motivational techniques

Coaching is appropriate for employees who can't seem to learn the new skills that they need in order to perform better. They are aware that there is a problem, but can't resolve it. They tend to perform in the same old unsatisfactory ways, even though they know this is ineffective. This often creates frustration. When you coach them, be aware that your nondirective approach may easily get an angry response.

Motivation is used for employees who have performed well, but seem to have stopped believing they

can succeed for some reason. Their performances may have only marginally dipped but they are disappointed. They need reassurance and motivation to overcome this temporary problem.

But people can react differently from the ways you expect. So be aware of some employees who will respond by feeling complacent, rather than by feeling encouraged.

It's easy to assume that both coaching and motivating are always appropriate. But coaching is appropriate for an employee who has not mastered the new skills, and motivating is appropriate for an employee with lapsed skills. This difference is important. If you try to motivate an employee who has never performed well, you are only offering false praise. If you coach an employee who has performed well, but is temporarily unsure of himself, you will only increase that uncertainty.

Coaching and motivating

Coaching

When an employee can't do what she is supposed to do, a motivational statement can seem absurd. What she needs is help on what she needs to do, not encouragement. Encouragement won't tell her how to behave and perform.

Example of coaching

An employee who can't write an accurate, succinct report needs support on how to write such a report. She needs coaching. No amount of motivational encouragement will help her to develop new skills.

Motivating

When an employee has previously performed to the required standard but his performance drops, he needs encouragement. He needs to be reminded that he has performed well and can do so again.

Example of motivating

An employee who can, and has, written accurate, succinct reports but is now failing to do so will feel disheartened. Motivation will remind her of her previous performance and refocus her mind on the skills she already has.

When you start to develop your employee, you'll need to decide whether coaching or motivating is a more appropriate technique.

Example: situations that clearly identify which technique should be used.

Henry

Henry never gets all of his work done even though he really tries hard. He is always behind even though he is very competent.

Henry needs coaching.

Mat

Mat has fallen behind. But he achieved his targets in previous weeks. He needs motivating.

When you start to coach, you'll employ some techniques that will help the employee to reflect and learn from her problematic performance. However, if the response is frustration and anger because the employee doesn't think you are directive enough, or because she is feeling guilty about her poor performance, you'll need to respond to get her to refocus on the task and take responsibility for her own.

Coaching and response to anger

Coach

You begin by encouraging the employee to reflect on the experience by asking her a simple question about progress, and then prompting her to think about the causes of the problem. You then ask the employee to consider how she should have behaved.

Responding to anger

Don't react by being directive or angry. Remind her that you are trying to get her to take responsibility, and that you are there to coach, not instruct. Prompt her with the different ways she could behave, and ask her which one she would choose and why.

Example: Henry responded angrily when Stacey started to coach him about his being persistently late finishing his work. Follow along.

Stacey: So, Henry, have you been able to get your work completed on time?

Henry: No, I've had real problems this week. I just can't seem to stop from getting distracted. I usually end up helping the other team members and then I'm behind again.

Stacey: Do you think you might get your work done if you didn't help them? Henry: If you don't want me to help the others, then why don't you just say so? As far as I'm concerned, it's good teamwork.

Stacey: Henry, how you choose to work is up to you. I'm not here to tell you what to do with every minute. You could offer to help after you've done your own work, or even get them to help you if you help them. Do you think either of those ideas would work?

Henry: Well, it would make sense to get my own work done first. I don't know if they'd actually be that eager to help me.

Stacey handles Henry in an exemplary way. She questions him to get him to reflect on his work, and then prompts him to think through why he is having difficulty. When he gets annoyed with her and suggests that she just tell him what he should do, she doesn't overreact.

Stacey calmly reminds him that it is his responsibility to organize his working day, and then gives him a couple of pertinent suggestions about how he might behave. She lets Henry reflect on the solution and come to his own conclusion.

Motivating employees who have problems is usually a case of getting them to take a measured look at their achievements and not to get dejected. But sometimes, this backfires and employees become complacent about their achievements. This means that they still have the problems but are less concerned about remedying them. In this case, you need to move to a more assertive form of motivation.

Motivating and dealing with a complacent response

Motivating

The basic approach is to give employees a summary report to reassure them that they shouldn't be so negative about their progress. This should specifically identify achievements. Making a comparison with behavior in the past can be very positive. Random flattery doesn't work.

Dealing with a complacent response

If employees exhibit a complacent response that suggests they have achieved as much as they can, don't agree with them. You should remind them that they are still having problems, and use any information you can about the desired behavioral targets to encourage them to work harder.

Example: Stacey faces this problem with Mat, another worker on her team with problems. He is dispirited by his seeming failure to meet his production target.

Mat: I fell behind again last week. I'm never going to meet the target. Stacey: Come on, Mat. You've shown a lot of improvement over the last few weeks. You're hitting your targets more and more every week.

Mat: It doesn't feel like that.

Stacey: Two months ago you hit your target 15 times. Last month it was over 20. You need to think about how far you've come.
Mat: Yeah, you're right. What am I worrying about? I've done pretty much what I'm supposed to.
Stacey: Wait a minute--you aren't there yet. You need to be hitting your performance target every day by the end of next month.
Mat: You're right. I'm going to work harder than ever this week.

Stacey motivates Mat by reminding him of his achievements and getting him to make comparisons. But when this results in a complacent attitude, she is quick to remind him of how far he still has to go.

Case Study: Question 1 of 4
Scenario

You are helping with the development of two of your employees - Maureen and Isabelle. Both have been given targets for performance improvement as part of being appraised. Neither of them is performing particularly well at the moment. Maureen has never been good at getting to know new people--she just withdraws from them. Isabelle has become less concerned about her punctuality, even though it had been improving.

Answer the questions, in order.

Question

How would you develop Maureen? What would be appropriate to say to her?

Options:

1. "Come on, Maureen. You can do it. I think you are really quite confident."
2. "You know that you can't expect customers to come to you. You won't make any sort of relationship with them like that."
3. "How's the relationship-building going at the moment?"
4. "So, is the problem that you don't know what to say to them?" 5. "What could you do to start a conversation?"

Answer

In fact, Maureen needs to be coached. Coaches should encourage reflection by simple questioning, prompt thinking about the causes of the problem, and help the employee to consider how she should have behaved.

Option 1: This is an incorrect option. You are trying to motivate Maureen. She needs to be coached because she has never managed to make relationships with others.

Option 2: This is an incorrect option. This is blaming Maureen. In coaching, your approach should be to ask questions so that she reflects and evaluates her own performance.

Option 3: This is a correct option. This question gently prompts Maureen to consider her performance. This is a good approach to starting a coaching interaction.

Option 4: This is a correct option. You have coached her by prompting Maureen to consider the causes of her problems with relationship building.

Option 5: This is a correct option. You have asked Maureen to consider how she should have behaved. This is a good coaching technique. You are helping Maureen to reflect on--and resolve--her own problems.

Case Study: Question 2 of 4
Scenario

You are helping with the development of two of your employees--Maureen and Isabelle. Both have been given targets for performance improvement as part of being appraised. Neither of them is performing particularly well at the moment. Maureen has never been good at getting to know new people--she just withdraws from them. Isabelle has become less concerned about her punctuality, even though it had been improving.

Answer the questions, in order.

Question

Maureen reacts angrily to you. She tells you that you it would be a lot quicker and easier if you just told her what to do. How should you respond to her?

Options:

1. "I'm not here to tell you what to do. Have you considered asking people about their families or vacations? Those are nice ways to start a conversation."
2. "I agree that it would be easier. But I don't know if you'd listen to me."
3. "You need to go up to people and ask them an easy, general question. The hardest part is

starting. Then, just listen and respond to what they say."

4. "What sort of introductory question would work best for you?"

Answer

Actually, to respond to Maureen's anger, you should remind her that her behavior is her responsibility. You should try to refocus her on the different ways she might behave to improve her performance.

Option 1: This is a correct option. Maureen needs to be reminded that you are trying to get her to take responsibility for her behavior. You should prompt her again to think of ways she could behave.

Option 2: This is an incorrect option. You should not respond to Maureen's anger with your own anger. A better technique would be to remind her that her behavior is her responsibility, and help her to think of better ways of performing.

Option 3: This is an incorrect option. This is instruction. Coaching Maureen should mean getting her to take responsibility for her own actions. You should support her to think of different ways she could perform.

Option 4: This is a correct option. A good technique to use when Maureen lost her temper is to try to get her to consider different options and to evaluate the usefulness of them.

Case Study: Question 3 of 4
Scenario

You are helping with the development of two of your employees - Maureen and Isabelle. Both have been given targets for performance improvement as part of being appraised. Neither of them is performing particularly well at the moment. Maureen has never been good at getting to know new people--she just withdraws from them. Isabelle has become less concerned about her punctuality, even though it had been improving.

Answer the questions, in order.

Question

How would you support Isabelle's development? What would you say to her?

Options:

1. "You have the best punctuality record in the company." 2. "You've been on time for most of the last month."
3. "Before you tried to fix this, you were late at least once a week. Now, it's no more than once a month." 4. "Have you thought about reorganizing your schedule?"

Answer

In fact, to motivate Isabelle you need to give her honest feedback on her progress, highlighting her achievements. You should support this with a comparison of a time she was not performing so well.

Option 1: This is an incorrect option. This is false flattery. It isn't justified by the facts, and Isabelle won't be motivated by it.

Option 2: This is a correct option. This is honest and genuine feedback. You have highlighted the good parts of her performance. This should help to motivate Isabelle.

Option 3: This is a correct option. By making this sort of comparison, you will help to show Isabelle that she has made progress. This should motivate her.

Option 4: This is an incorrect option. This is coaching Isabelle. She has been punctual in the past. She needs more motivational support.

Case Study: Question 4 of 4

Scenario

You are helping with the development of two of your employees--Maureen and Isabelle. Both have been given targets for performance improvement as part of being appraised. Neither of them is performing particularly well at the moment. Maureen has never been good at getting to know new people--she just withdraws from them. Isabelle has become less concerned about her punctuality, even though it had been improving.

Answer the questions, in order.

Question

Isabelle starts to suggest that she can manage her time easily, and that it's not really something she needs to worry about or try very hard at. What should you say to her in response?

Options:

1. "Don't forget, your target is to be late no more than twice a month."
2. "That's right. You've got your punctuality back on track now."
3. "You've improved a lot, but you were still late twice last week."
4. "Have you thought about keeping a time log to see where the problem is?"

Answer

Actually, you can defuse Isabelle's complacency by reminding her of the overall target and helping her to remember that she is still having some problems.

Option 1: This is a correct option. You should defuse Isabelle's complacency by reminding her of her overall target. This will stop her from being falsely self-assured and keep her motivated.

Option 2: This is an incorrect option. Agreeing with Isabelle will only increase her complacency. You should put her achievements in perspective and remind her what she needs to do to meet her target.

Option 3: This is a correct option. Isabelle must be reminded of the problems she is having if she is to avoid complacency.

Option 4: This is an incorrect option. You are coaching Isabelle. She needs to be motivated. She has been punctual in the past - this is a temporary problem.

Maureen's problems with developing relationships can be helped by coaching her. You should use some simple questions to get her to reflect on her problems, and then encourage her to think through possible solutions. When she responds angrily, because she wants you to be more directive, you should remind her that you are trying to coach her. You should get her to consider some options for improving her performance and evaluate their usefulness for her.

Isabelle's lack of motivation can be resolved by honest feedback about her progress supplemented with comparisons, so that she can see how far she has progressed. Her complacency needs to be controlled by reminding her of the problems she has had and how far she has to go to achieve her overall target.

The best way to support your team is by being a coach and a motivator. Both skills are essential if you're going to get employees to take responsibility for their actions and keep trying as hard as they can through difficult times.

Maximize the effectiveness of training programs

For some managers, any sort of training equals development. They think that their responsibility for supporting the development of employees is fulfilled by sending them on the next available training course.

But they are wrong. Training is a useful part of developing an employee if it is specifically designed to help that employee improve performance.

Monique's method of developing her team was simple. She enrolled them in training courses. That way, she could check development off her list and forget about it. She put Francis on a people skills course because it was pretty similar to the conflict management training he needed. She arranged for Alice to take a course on the theory of database design when she needed training on how to use one. She had Pete take a training course about the new accounting software even though he didn't have a copy on his desktop computer yet.

In fact, she was using training as a development tool entirely inappropriately. Francis's course was too general, Alice's course was too theoretical, and Pete could not apply any of the learning from his course.

If training is to be an effective development tool, it must follow three rules. It must be:
- specifically focused on the employee's development needs,
- designed to give the employee new skills that she can use,
- followed by immediate opportunities to practice the new skills in real work situations.

As a manager, you are responsible for ensuring that the training courses you enroll your people in follow these three rules. If Monique had done so, the training she organized for her team members would have been very different.

Bow should a development opportunity be addressed

Francis

Francis was OK when everyone was friendly, but had problems when handling any form of conflict. Monique found a course for experienced supervisors who had this type of problem. It was full of role plays and gave him every chance to develop the new skills he needed.

Alice

Monique enrolled Alice in a two-part introduction to using a database course. The first part concentrated on basic operations and then Alice was assigned some practical tasks to complete back at work. The second part of the course covered more advanced procedures with more work-based tasks.

Pete

Monique didn't enroll Pete in the first available course about using the new software. She waited until it had been installed on his computer and then enrolled him immediately. The hands-on practice in the course enabled him to use the software as soon as he got back to work.

You might imagine that effective training is a daunting experience for a manager who only has to arrange training for employees occasionally. But, in fact, the rules are very easy to apply if you follow these simple guidelines.

Focused

A simple and effective way to keep the training correctly focused is to answer the following question. What is it that the individual needs to be able to do that he isn't able to do now? You only need to match the training to these objectives.

Example of focused

If you have an employee who needs to be able to counsel poorly performing team members, look for training where learners will practice counseling skills. If learners get to use their own scenarios, that's even better.

Practical

Find out whether the training is geared to practical use of skills or if it is more theoretical in its approach. Lean toward training that is weighted toward job-related skills. You should be looking for role plays, practical exercises, simulations, and case studies.

Example of practical

Ensure that your employee has the opportunity to apply the skills in a real work situation, as soon as possible after returning from training. You must consider resources, time, support, and feedback on the newly applied performance skills.

Opportunities

If the training is on designing a database, look for sessions within the training in which learners will actually be designing a database to use in work. Courses where learners must bring work- related information with them add an extra practical dimension.

Example of Opportunities

If you have employees who need to attend a "Managing without Authority" course, this should ideally be scheduled for two weeks before they start to manage their next project. Then, they'll get to practice their new skills back in the workplace.

By following these guidelines, training is more particular and specific to the employee. It is more useful and is immediately integrated into everyday working practices.

Example: how Colin used a guideline to develop effective training for Serena

focused

Colin defined the training objective for Serena as, "to be able to interview potential new hires." This was exactly what he wanted her to do. She hadn't interviewed anyone before. He wanted her to be capable of conducting recruitment interviews on her own.

practical

Colin spoke to the trainer for the assertiveness course. He identified that each session contained at least one role play. Each learner would have to conduct an interview in the way the course taught. The role play interview was for a job that Serena would need to recruit for in the near future.

opportunities

Colin gave Serena three interviews to manage after her training course. He set aside some time so that she could prepare herself thoroughly for each interview. He interviewed alongside her and was able to give her feedback on the way she handled the interviews.

x

Activity - **Planning Training Opportunities for Development**

Identify someone on your team who has a training need. Then complete the following activity to help you improve the effectiveness of your team member's training.

Part 1 – to be completed before the training takes place

1) Record well-defined training objectives

Decide what you want your team member to be able to do as a result of the training. Examples are inputting customer data onto a new database, operating a new piece of machinery, or achieving defined customer service targets.

Also decide when you expect the team member to realistically achieve this objective.

Make a note of what the training objective is and the date by which you expect the learner to be able to achieve the objective.

2) Ensure the training will provide the learner with the actual skills required in work

Before enrolling the employee in a course, ensure that the training includes role plays, simulations, and/or practical sessions that will enable learners to apply the skills they are developing.

Make a note of what the practical activities that the training will include.

3) Ensure that resources, time, and support will be available for learners to put their learning into practice when they return from their training

Before the training event, you should both agree on what the learner will need in order to achieve the expected outcome of the training. This may mean that some of the learner's regular work is allocated to another team member, or that necessary equipment is made available.

Make a note of the resources, time, and support that you have agreed on to ensure that they are available to learners when they return from their training.

Part 2 – to be completed after the training has taken place

1) Agree on a time to evaluate the effectiveness of the training with the learner

This should be on, or very shortly after, the date you expected the learner to have achieved the training objective.

2) At the meeting, answer the following questions

To what extent has the learner achieved the training objective? Include descriptions of any aspects that have been exceeded or missed.

Did the training include the activities specified above?

Were the activities included in the training sufficient for the learner to apply the required skills back in the workplace? If not, what else would have helped?

Were the agreed on resources, time, and support available following the training? If so, were they sufficient for the learner to achieve the learning objectives? If not, what else would have helped?

Do you or the learner need to do anything now to ensure the training objective is met?

Learning Aids - **Disciplinary Checklist**

Is there evidence of persistent failure? This is failure to achieve agreed on targets/standards on at least two occasions.

Is there evidence of action to support the employee to improve? For example, training, coaching or increased supervision.

Is the anticipated disciplinary response in line with the stated disciplinary policy of the company?

Has such a possible response to the poor performance been clearly indicated to the employee?

Is the response comparable to similar incidents of poor performance within the company?

Learning Aid - **Sharon's Appraisal Notes**

Month	Issue	Action
July	5 percent below target cold calls; 15 percent below target follow-up visits	Talked to Sharon. No apparent reason for slow down. Sharon aware of the problem and will try harder.
Aug	Both targets just met	Congratulated Sharon on improvement. She promised to maintain standard from now on.
Sept	10 percent below target cold calls; 10 percent below target follow-up visits	Listened in on Sharon's calls and suggested that she use a more direct, assertive approach. Emphasized need to sound enthusiastic and respond quickly to customer cues.
Oct	5 percent below target cold calls; on target follow-up visits	Congratulated Sharon on improvement and emphasized need to continue. Explained that we would put her on a lower salary scale if this level of performance did not continue.
Nov	10 percent below target cold calls; 5 percent below target follow-up visits	Enrolled Sharon in refresher course
Dec	10 percent below target cold calls; 5 percent below target follow-up visits	Reemphasized warning and possible lowering of pay scale.

Learning aid - **Effective Appraisal**
Stage 1
Set the scene for the meeting by:
- explaining how you will run the meeting
- taking control with firm, precise statements
- telling – not asking – the appraisee how the meeting will be organized
- if the appraisee challenges you over the direction of the meeting, be firm and insist on your approach

Stage 2
Complete the evaluation of the appraisee using the forms provided. Create a calm and controlled dialogue with the appraisee by:

- starting with areas of agreement before moving to areas of disagreement between your evaluation of the appraisee and his self-evaluation
- listening and responding to any points the appraisee may make
- finalizing the evaluation stage by reiterating the decisions you have made

Stage 3

State the final outcome of the appraisal in terms of any development of the employee's skills you have decided upon. Do this by:

- adopting a positive enthusiastic tone about future developments
- motivating the employee to take part in future developments
- emphasizing the specific and individual nature of the development to make employees feel that it is specifically targeted at them

Learning aid - Annual Broadcast Project
The Broadcast

The company produces The Broadcast. A project group drawn from representatives across the company is convened six months before the publication date to produce The Broadcast. The group operates as a series of small teams with specific tasks. Some individual tasks are also defined.

- Six weeks before publication, someone has to contact and arrange for each department head to provide a 1,000-word article on the main achievement of his department.

- One person has to keep the accounts for The Broadcast.
- One person has to persuade each senior executive to donate a prize to the crossword competition in the magazine.
- A small team is designated to procure external advertising by contacting every customer and supplier of the company to try to persuade them to take out as much advertising space as possible.
- Another team has to agree on the layout of The Broadcast. There are inevitably strong disagreements as departments vie with each other to be given the most coverage. The team has to reach a collective decision on this and stick to it.
- The third team has to organize the "Employee of the Year" award. Departments are asked for nominations three weeks before the publication date and this team has to decide who is to be selected for interviewing, conduct the interviews, and select the person in time to write a profile of them for The Broadcast.

The development needs of Greg, Tara, and Alicia are summarized here as follows:

Greg

Greg is a very experienced designer. His expertise lies in using Computer-aided Design (CAD). Greg, however, is very unassuming about his skills and knowledge, and keeps a low profile in the department. You feel that you are not using him to his full potential. You want him to take a more assertive leadership role with the younger designers. You feel he should be giving them more advice and direction, particularly in relation to CAD. You have tried to get him to mentor some of the new hires but he seems to leave them on their own quickly, even though they are prone to making mistakes.

Tara

Tara's role as an administrative assistant used to suit her. It involved a lot of detailed individual working and little interaction with other people. But the role has changed and she now has to arrange interviews in the company. This involves meeting and greeting prospective applicants, and showing them around. She also has to attend recruitment events and actively encourage young graduates to think about joining the company. Tara is shy and finds these demands very difficult. She has asked you to help her to try and overcome her shyness.

Alicia

Alicia is very unpopular as the assistant team leader in the marketing department. But she doesn't know it. She decides on where to place ads. All the team members have strong opinions about this but she doesn't even consult them. She is abrasive and very sure of herself, and if any team members try to make some suggestions about where to place ads, she shouts them down. She says that it is her job to decide. The rest of the team has told you that unless Alicia starts discussing the placement of ads with them, they are going to seek transfers. You want to get Alicia to develop a less confrontational approach to managing other people.

CHAPTER THREE

Glossary and Bibliography

Glossary

A

Autonomy - The employee's right to perform a task in the way he chooses.

B

Behaviorally based rating scales - These are detailed descriptions of the behaviors an employee shows during performance. Often, the behavior is listed from excellent attributes, through required attributes, to behavior that does not enhance performance.

F

Forced distribution scale - This is when percentages of scores must be apportioned to various sequential categories. For example, 20 percent must be excellent, 60 percent must be good, and 20 percent must be poor performers.

I

Individual factors - These are differing individual aptitudes and capacities that affect performance.

J

Job description - A written statement listing the elements of a particular job or occupation.

P

Performance goals - Performance goals are also referred to as performance objectives. Performance goals identify what an organization wants as an outcome from a job task or activity performed by an employee.

Performance log - A log--often just in note form--of a manager's observations about the performances of his team members.

Performance plan - The outcome of a discussion between the manager and employee, which defines and sets performance goals.

R

Rating scales - A numerical scoring system to assess performance.

Raw data - Data which has not been reviewed or modified.

S

Self-directed Teams - Self-directed teams are teams which operate with less management and supervisory involvement, and determine their own objectives.

Self-rating - When an employee is asked to rate her own performance.

Status report - A formal report from an employee to a manager indicating performance progress.

System factors - Factors produced by an ineffective working system that are beyond the control of individuals.

T

Telecommuting - Working from home for some or all of the week and communicating electronically with the main office.

Bibliography
1. *Stress-free Performance Appraisals: Turn Your Most Painful Management Duty into a Powerful Motivational Tool* - Armstrong, Sharon and Madelyn Appelbaum, Career Press, 2003
2. *Abolishing Performance Appraisals: Why They Backfire and What to Do Instead* - Coens, Tom and Mary Jenkins, Berrett-Koehler Publishers, 2000
3. *Appraisal: Routes to Improved Performance* - Fletcher, Clive, 1993
4. *Performance Appraisals: How to Achieve Top Results* - Glidden, Priscilla A. and Karen S. Whelan, 1996
5. *The Performance Appraisal Question and Answer Book* - Grote, Dick, 2002
6. *Performance Improvement Interventions: Enhancing People, Processes, and Organizations through Performance Technology* - Van Tiem, Darlene M, James L. Moseley and Joan Conway Dessinger, 2001
7. *Managing Performance: Building Accountability for Organizational Success* - http://www.ddiworld.com
8. *Performance Appraisals Don't Work* - http://humanresources.about.com

www.ingramcontent.com/pod-product-compliance
Lightning Source LLC
Chambersburg PA
CBHW020907180526
45163CB00007B/2657